THE PACIFIC RIM

EAST ASIA AT THE DAWN OF A NEW CENTURY

ELAINE PASCOE

Twenty-First Century Books
Brookfield, Connecticut

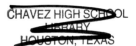

ACKNOWLEDGMENTS

The author thanks Agnes Brackman, for her invaluable research assistance, and Patricia Culleton, for her patience and professionalism as editor of this book.

Cover photograph courtesy of Science Source/Photo Researchers, Inc. (© Tom Van Sant.) Photographs courtesy of Liaison Agency, Inc.: pp. 12 (© Wolfgang Kaehler), 42 (© Wolfgang Kaehler), 60 (© David Hartung), 82 (© Wolfgang Kaehler), 94 (© Joe Lynch), 112 (© Alexis Duclos); Woodfin Camp & Associates: pp. 24 (© Mike Yamashita), 70 (© Nathan Benn). Maps by Joe LeMonnier.

Library of Congress Cataloging-in-Publication Data
Pascoe, Elaine.
The Pacific rim: East Asia at the dawn of a new
century / by Elaine Pascoe.
p.   cm.
Includes bibliographical references (p.   ) and index.
Summary: examines the history and current economic and political importance of Japan, China, Taiwan, the Koreas, Southeast Asia, Indonesia, and Malaysia.
ISBN 0-7613-3015-1 (lib. bdg.)
1. East Asia—History—Juvenile literature. 2. East Asia—Economic conditions—Juvenile literature. 3. East Asia—Politics and government—Juvenile literature. 4. Asia, Southeastern—History—Juvenile literature. 5. Asia, Southeastern—Economic conditions—Juvenile literature. 6. Asia, Southeastern—Politics and government—Juvenile literature. [1. East Asia. 2. Asia, Southeastern.] I. Title
DS511.P35   1999
950.4'29—dc21   98-28556   CIP   AC

Published by Twenty-First Century Books
A Division of The Millbrook Press, Inc.
2 Old New Milford Road
Brookfield, Connecticut 06804

CONTENTS

THE PACIFIC RIM

INTRODUCTION

When Americans look abroad, they are used to looking east—across the Atlantic Ocean, toward Europe. The reasons are historical. Most Americans trace their roots to one part of Europe or another. For centuries, Europe was the world's center of wealth and power, and European nations controlled vast empires. Even in the twentieth century, as those empires fell apart and the United States assumed a leading role in world affairs, Americans continued to focus on Europe.

While Americans were looking east, however, new powers were rising. Beginning in the 1960s, the nations of East Asia experienced spectacular economic growth. Japan led the way. Fueled by exports of cars and high-tech products, its economy grew to be the second largest in the world, after that of the United States. Hong Kong, Singapore, Taiwan, and South Korea were quick to follow Japan's lead. Other nations, including Thailand, Indonesia, Malaysia, and the Philippines weren't far behind these new "Asian tigers," as the fast-growing East Asian nations were called. Even the region's Communist nations, seeing the success of their neighbors, began to open their markets and permit free trade, at least to a degree. China, which as the world's most populous nation would rank as a major power by virtue of size alone, began to develop its huge economic potential.

The export-driven success of the Asian tigers was the envy of the West. Foreign investment poured in, financing everything from airports to skyscrapers. As the wealth of East Asian nations grew, so did their political influence. By the 1990s many people were predicting that the twenty-first century would be the Pacific Century because Asia's rising strength would shift the balance of world power from the Atlantic to the Pacific Ocean. Then came a reversal that cast that prediction in a new light. In 1997 the effects of too much building, too much spending, and especially too much borrowing began to hit home in East Asia. The trouble started in Thailand in July, when a slowdown in economic growth triggered a speculative run on the nation's currency. The government was forced to devalue the currency, and that made it impossible for banks and businesses to repay loans obtained in dollars and yen. Foreign investors began to pull out, sending the Thai economy and currency into a tailspin. In a ripple effect, the trouble spread to other East Asian nations, which experienced the same dizzying cycle of falling currency and stock market values. Businesses closed, and workers lost their jobs. The International Monetary Fund (IMF) came to the rescue in the worst cases—Indonesia and South Korea, as well as Thailand—with loans and reform measures aimed at curbing the practices that led to the crisis. Economists forecast a long recession for the region, and most expected worldwide repercussions.

The 1997 events were a setback, but one that many people thought would be temporary. The Asian tigers and their neighbors were down but not out, and most analysts still expected the Pacific Rim to thrive in the coming years. Still, the economic crisis highlighted some of the problems that affected the countries of East Asia even before their incredible boom was cut short. Lax regulation of business, corruption and cronyism, authoritarian rule—to one degree or another, in several countries, these and other problems helped set the stage for economic disaster.

The Pacific Ocean laps at the shores of many nations. The major Pacific Rim nations include the United States, Canada, and Mexico on the eastern side of the ocean and Australia and New Zealand on the southwest. The focus in this book, however, is on the East Asian nations that are positioned to influence events in the twenty-first century—through economic and political leadership, or through a potential for conflict. Americans are familiar with their neighbors, Canada and Mexico. They share language and cultural traditions with Australia and New Zealand. But many know little about the Asian Pacific countries.

Relations between the United States and many of the Asian Pacific countries have not always been smooth. In the twentieth century, Americans have fought three wars in East Asia, while Asian immigrants to the United States have often encountered extraordinary prejudice. Prejudice and lack of interest have kept many Americans from learning much about the Asian Pacific nations, which have cultural traditions very different from those of the United States and European countries—and quite different from one another.

Ignorance about these countries will handicap Americans in the years to come. To participate in the future of the Pacific Rim, Americans must turn their focus to the west and learn to understand the region. A single book can't hope to cover the rich variety and long history of the Asian Pacific countries. This volume is intended to serve as an introduction to selected nations and to some of the issues and problems that will confront them in the twenty-first century.

RUSSIA

Sea of
Okhotsk

MONGOLIA

CHINA

N. KOREA

S. KOREA

JAPAN

PACIFIC
OCEAN

TAIWAN

LAOS

THAILAND

CAMBODIA   VIETNAM

PHILIPPINES

MALAYSIA

SINGAPORE

INDONESIA

NDIAN

OCEAN

AUSTRALIA

LOOKING WEST

EAST ASIA IN AMERICAN EYES

In 1784 the merchant ship *Empress of China* sailed from New York City to Canton (Guang-zhou), China, and returned bearing teas, spices, and other luxuries for the American market. This trip, which hardly seems remarkable today, was a significant step for the new United States. Until Americans won their independence in the Revolutionary War, they had been barred by Britain from trading directly with other countries. The voyage of the *Empress of China* marked the start of what quickly became a thriving trade. It was also the start of a long period of mutual misunderstanding and culture shock between Americans on the one hand and the Chinese and other Asian peoples on the other.

THE CHINA TRADE

American trading ships were soon calling regularly at Canton and at other Asian ports. Manila, in the Spanish-controlled Philippines, was opened to trade in 1796. By the 1820s, Americans were doing brisk business at Manila, exchanging U.S.-made goods for spices, sugar, hemp, and other products from the islands. Fortunes were made in East Asian trade throughout the 1800s. At first, most ships sailed from ports on the U.S. East Coast, across the Atlantic Ocean, and around the Cape of Good Hope at the southern tip of Africa to reach China and neighboring lands. That route was long, but less risky than the

A BRONZE LION IS ON GUARD IN BEIJING'S ANCIENT FORBIDDEN CITY, WHICH CONTAINS HUNDREDS OF BUILDINGS, INCLUDING THE IMPERIAL PALACES OF THE EMPERORS OF CHINA FROM 1421 TO 1911.

other choice—around stormy and dangerous Cape Horn, at the tip of South America, and across the Pacific Ocean. But speed meant profit in the China trade, and traders increasingly were willing to take the risk. In the 1840s and 1850s, American merchant traders launched some of the fastest sailing ships ever built, the magnificent square-rigged clipper ships, and sent them around Cape Horn to China. The clippers cut the voyage time from four months to three.

Almost three hundred years earlier, European explorers and settlers had begun coming to America in search of three things: gold, land, and fast routes to China. Now the same lures helped draw Americans west. By the mid-1800s, the United States had extended its territory to California. San Francisco, perhaps the finest port on the North American Pacific Coast, was now an American city, and the United States was well placed to play a leading role in the growing trade between Asia and the West. In 1853 American commodore Matthew Perry arrived in Japan determined to establish relations. Although the initial goal was to get permission for American ships to refuel and take refuge in Japanese ports, trade developed in the years that followed.

Reports brought back by traders and sailors colored American views of East Asia. Seen through their eyes, China was truly exotic—so many Chinese ways were directly opposite American ways. Chinese men wore silk robes and kept their hair in long braided queues. Women, in contrast, wore trousers—something no American woman of the time would dream of doing—and women's feet were bound tightly in childhood so that they would stay small. The Chinese language was unintelligible to Americans. It had no alphabet and was written "backward," from right to left.

Other differences deeply shocked Americans. The Chinese considered female children next to worthless, and many girls were killed at birth or, when they were old enough, sold as servants. A man could have several wives or concubines, as long as he could afford to support them. In parts of China, people ate dogs. Word of these practices helped convince Americans that the Chinese were backward and barbaric. Confirming the view was the fact that the Chinese worshipped many different gods, as followers of Buddhism, Taoism, and other ancient religions. Many Americans of the time believed that only Christians could be truly civilized. Moreover, the Chinese were ruled by an all-powerful emperor, another contrast to the democratic United States.

To the Chinese, however, it was the Americans and other Westerners who were backward. The Chinese empire was in full flower in the 1700s. The government, mistrustful of these barbarians, at first restricted American traders to the port of Canton, and later to foreign sections of a few other ports. Only a handful of Americans saw anything of the vast country beyond, so they remained ignorant of China as anything but a source of tea and luxuries. Nor, for the most part, did they care to learn more. A seaman on the clipper ship *Sea Serpent*, after a day at liberty in Shanghai, wrote: "I was glad enough to get aboard again towards evening, for the streets were so very filthy and the Chinamen such a miserable-looking set of beings that one soon got disgusted with the shore."[1]

THE MISSIONARIES

For a number of Americans, Asia became more than a source of goods and profits, however. Missionaries fixed on the region, especially China, Korea, and Japan, with the goal of Christianizing and "civilizing" the people there. They went as preachers, but also as teachers, doctors, and advocates of America's democratic way of life. Protestant denominations supported their work through missionary societies, and the missionaries reported back by sending regular newsletters and by lecturing to church groups when they returned to the United States. Thus their views, too, helped shape America's picture of Asia.

The first American missionaries to China arrived in Canton in 1830. (European Catholic missionaries had already been in China for some time.) They didn't meet with much success—it took them eighteen years to win their first converts. Missionaries, like traders, were at first restricted to a handful of ports; later, they won rights to set up missions, schools, and clinics in villages throughout much of China. The missionaries had good intentions, and medical missions in particular were truly helpful to Chinese peasants and workers, who had little or no other access to health care. The schools they established brought learning to a wide range of people, including women, who had previously had little opportunity for education. In this way Western science and technology, and Western ideas of democracy and social justice, slowly began to take root in China.

But many missionaries lacked understanding of and sympathy for the Chinese. The missionaries tended to live in walled compounds, and most did not learn the Chinese language. Frustration was common. "I am afraid that nothing short of the Society for the Diffusion of Cannon Balls will give [the Chinese] the useful knowledge they now require to realize their own helplessness," one missionary wrote in 1858. "They are among the most craven of people, cruel and selfish as heathenism can make men."[2] Not all missionaries were so unsympathetic, but even those who weren't tended to view Asians as inferiors. And if American missionaries misunderstood and mistrusted the Chinese, the "compliment" was returned. Foreigners were viewed with suspicion by many Chinese and sometimes pelted with dirt and stones in the streets. Sometimes they were killed. In the 1870 Tientsin Massacre, rioters killed twenty-one foreigners, among them ten nuns.

Japan fared slightly better in American perceptions, thanks largely to a number of American teachers who worked there in the mid- to late 1800s. Through their writings, and in lectures back in the United States, they helped Americans appreciate Japanese art and culture. The Japanese likewise were taken with American ways, especially American technology. Despite the mutual admiration, however, most Americans had a superficial and romanticized view of Japan as being a land of cherry blossoms and graceful women in silk kimonos.

As for other East Asian cultures, Americans knew little or nothing about them. This wasn't surprising. The United States was not yet the world power it is today, and through the 1800s Americans were concerned with matters closer to home—the issue of slavery, the Civil War, the settling of the West.

IMMIGRATION

Other factors contributed to the picture Americans held of East Asia. Chinese immigrants began to arrive in California in the mid-1800s, drawn (like so many others) by the discovery of gold there in 1848. By the end of the 1860s there were 63,000 Chinese in America. Nearly all were men. Many were contract laborers, "coolies," who helped build railroads and performed other hard jobs at wages below those of Americans. Others opened laundries, restaurants, and similar businesses in the mining towns of the West, where there were few women to provide such services.

Like Americans in China, Chinese in America tended to live apart, and most spoke little English. There was no need to learn American ways—they planned to get rich and return to China. Even later, when Chinese immigrants established families and began to put down roots in their new country, they had a difficult time winning acceptance. The Chinese met greater prejudice than other immigrant groups. Workers feared that low-wage Chinese labor would put them out of their jobs. Moreover, the Chinese looked different, worshipped "heathen" gods, and spoke a language Americans found outlandish. Many Americans viewed all Chinese as shifty, devious, and dishonest. Resentment reached a peak in the 1880s, when Chinese immigration was suspended. By then, Japanese immigrants had begun to arrive and encounter the same level of prejudice.

In fact, many Americans saw no difference between the Chinese and Japanese—both were part of a Yellow Peril that threatened the United States.

REGIONAL POWERS

Balancing this view was a growing appreciation of Asia's potential as a market. In the early years of the China trade, merchants had struggled to find products they could exchange for the Asian luxuries Americans craved. U.S. ships carried sea-otter pelts, Mexican silver, and Turkish opium to China, and returned with tea, silk, and porcelain. By the end of the nineteenth century, however, the United States was becoming an industrial nation. People in Asian countries were customers for American products that ranged from steel to sewing machines.

The United States was also becoming a major power, with an army and navy prepared to protect its interests worldwide. When the United States took control of Puerto Rico and the Philippines following the Spanish-American War in 1898, it seemed that the country might one day acquire a global colonial empire, like the British Empire. Americans generally felt that their country had much to offer the rest of the world—that it could, and should, lead other nations to the ideal of democracy. But most Americans were uncomfortable with the idea of empire, and the U.S. focus remained economic. To many Americans, the Philippines were valuable mainly as a base from which to expand Asian trade.

The emergence of the United States as a world power came at a time when there were important changes in East Asia, partly as a result of contact with the West. In China the Manchu emperors, who had ruled since the middle of the seventeenth century, were losing their grip on the country. As the government grew weaker, it relied increasingly on foreign nations for support. This opened the way for Britain and other European nations to establish what were called spheres of interest on Chinese territory, through agreements and leases. Within these regions, the European powers granted mining, railway, and other concessions to their citizens, and they brought in soldiers to protect their interests.

The United States did not try to follow the European lead in China. Instead, it adopted what became known as the Open Door policy. This was initially a request for the Europeans to grant all nations the same trading rights they themselves enjoyed within their individual spheres of interest. President William McKinley, who was behind the policy, hoped it would allow the nation to enjoy the benefits of Asian trade without committing troops or resources to maintain a presence in

China. Nevertheless, Americans were drawn in when the Boxer Rebellion, an antiforeign uprising, broke out in 1900. McKinley's stated goals for joining the European powers in crushing the rebellion were to restore order, preserve trading rights, and prevent China from collapsing. By taking part, the United States also helped deter the Europeans from carving up Chinese territory among themselves once the revolt ended.

Japan, meanwhile, was becoming a modern industrial nation and an important regional power. Japan delivered a stinging defeat to China in the Sino-Japanese War of 1895, a fight over which country would control Korea. In 1904–1905 the Japanese beat the Russians in another fight over regional influence. President Theodore Roosevelt helped negotiate an end to that conflict and won the Nobel Peace Prize for doing so. Roosevelt had good reasons for playing the role of peacemaker—he hoped that the U.S. presence in the Pacific would expand, and it was not in American interests to have either Russia or Japan in control of the region.

Japan's victories surprised many people in the West, who were impressed with the efficiency of the Japanese forces. Americans in particular, since they were seeking to establish their own place in Asia, began to see Japan as a threat. Writers and commentators discussed Japanese "militarism," and resentment grew against Japanese and other Asian immigrants. In 1924 the United States closed the door to Asian immigration and denied Asians the right to become U.S. citizens.

SHIFTING VIEWS

The Boxer Rebellion was a prelude to the turmoil that would sweep China in the twentieth century, as revolution and civil war divided the country. In much the same way, Japan's growing power marked the start of a course of events that would lead ultimately to World War II. Later chapters will cover these and other major developments of the twentieth century. All have helped shape American views of Asia at a time when the United States has been increasingly focused on the Pacific—politically, economically, and militarily.

American attitudes have undergone a series of abrupt reversals in the twentieth century. During World War II, Japan was America's enemy; China was Japan's victim and a U.S. ally. After Communists came to power in China in 1949, Americans saw China as a threat; Japan, occupied by U.S. troops and reconstructed on the American democratic model, was now a friend. The threat of communism led to U.S. involvement in two Asian wars—in Korea and Vietnam—and dominated American perceptions and policies through the 1980s.

But even after more than two hundred years of contact, the driving force underlying relations between the United States and other Pacific nations remains trade, just as it was when the *Empress of China* set sail in 1784. Today Americans view Asia as a region with enormous potential—and the ability to affect the world economy.

JAPAN
NEW PRESSURES IN ASIA'S POWERHOUSE

n Tokyo and other major Japanese cities, bars and restaurants are crowded late into the night. A quick check of the tables shows that the patrons are mostly groups of businessmen. They've already put in a long day at the office; now, they're out eating and drinking with their coworkers. They seem to be having fun, although in truth many of them would rather be home with their families at this late hour. But not joining associates after work would be unthinkable—the sort of blunder that could ruin a career. The *sarariman* (salary men), as businessmen are called, will straggle home late, catch a few hours of sleep, and be back at work early the next morning for another long day.

Since the end of World War II, Japan has transformed itself from a defeated nation into an economic powerhouse. Its success was so impressive that in the 1980s people around the world sought to analyze the factors in Japanese society that produced it, so they could emulate them. They found much to admire, especially in the way the Japanese seemed to apply traditional community values—such as placing group goals over personal needs—to the modern business world. But in the 1990s, it became clear that Japan was not immune to the economic and social problems that other countries face, and that holding to traditional ways might not be the best approach to solving them.

MAJOR CITIES IN JAPAN EXPANDED RAPIDLY AFTER WORLD WAR II. MORE THAN 80 PERCENT OF THE PEOPLE LIVE IN CROWDED URBAN AREAS, SUCH AS THIS ONE IN OSAKA.

POPULATION PRESSURE

Japan is one of the most densely populated countries on earth. Altogether, the four large islands and many smaller ones that make up the country have less land than the state of Montana. Yet roughly 126 million people live in Japan—almost half the population of the United States. Imagine what Montana would be like if every American now living west of Kansas City moved there, and you have an idea of how crowded Japan is. Japan isn't the ethnic melting pot that the United States is, however. As an ethnic group, the Japanese have changed little since the third century, even as their country has changed dramatically.

Japan is a nation of cities—more than 80 percent of the people live in urban areas. This is a recent development; cities grew incredibly fast in the years after World War II, and they continue to grow. Most of the major cities, including Tokyo, Yokohama, Osaka, and Kyoto, are on Honshu, the largest island. The smaller islands of Kyushu and Shikoku, separated from Honshu by the calm waters of the Inland Sea, are also densely populated. The northern island of Hokkaido, with its rugged terrain and harsh winters, is less crowded. Even so, its population is growing rapidly. Living space throughout Japan is at a premium, and most homes are small. In cities, traditional wooden houses have largely given way to apartment buildings.

Agricultural land is at a premium, too. Only about 15 percent of Japan's total area is suitable for farming. Much of the rest is mountainous and forested, justly celebrated for its beauty but too rugged for agriculture. To make the most of the available land, Japanese farmers have terraced hillsides to create rice fields. Except on Hokkaido, there isn't enough open pasture to raise cattle and other grazing livestock. Japan has turned to the sea to feed its people, and today it ranks as one of the leading fishing nations in the world. Even so, the country must import large quantities of food.

Likewise, Japan has little in the way of minerals, except for some coal. It relies on imported supplies of oil and gas, although it also generates electricity at hydro-electric and nuclear power plants. Yet its factories hum around the clock, turning raw materials into everything from steel and automobiles to silk cloth and computer chips. Japan's economy is fueled by foreign trade. It relies on imports to keep its industries running, and its products find markets worldwide.

YEARS OF CHANGE

Like other island nations, once-isolated Japan found wealth and power overseas. Japan's influence in the world is so widespread that it's difficult to believe how recently this nation took a place on the international stage. A country with historical and cultural traditions that reach back over many centuries, Japan was virtually closed to the rest of the world until less than 150 years ago. But once its isolation ended, the country transformed itself rapidly, becoming Asia's dominant military power in the early twentieth century and, after defeat in World War II, rebounding to become an economic superpower.

The transformation began within fifteen years of Commodore Perry's 1853 visit. For centuries leading up to that time, Japan had been nominally ruled by an emperor—but in fact controlled by shoguns, a series of military rulers who governed in the emperor's name. It was they who had barred foreigners from the country, ensuring peace and security at the cost of isolation. The start of trade with the West, however small at first, heightened class conflicts and divisions between traditionalists and those who wanted the country to modernize. In 1868 the shogunate was toppled, and power was placed directly in the hands of Emperor Mutsuhito, who would rule until 1912. He took the name Meiji, or "enlightened rule," and the era that followed is generally known as the Meiji Period.

It was a time of headlong change. A group of determined government officials guided the emperor and pushed Japan into the modern era, building factories, port facilities, railways, and a telegraph system. They established the foundation of a national school system, through university levels, that was open to all people, regardless of their income. They also reorganized Japan's armed forces, creating a powerful army and navy equipped with modern weapons. In less than 30 years, the country went from international backwater to international power.

In case anyone doubted Japan's new muscle, its armed forces defeated China, in the Sino-Japanese War of 1895, and Russia, in the Russo-Japanese War of 1904–1905. At issue in both these conflicts was control of the Korean peninsula. The kingdom of Korea was the foreign nation closest to Japan; moreover, the peninsula guarded the southern straits leading into the Sea of Japan. To the Japanese, control of the peninsula was a matter of national security. But so it was to the Chinese, and the Russians looked on Korea as a place to expand their influence in East Asia. By defeating both powers, Japan was able to control and ultimately annex Korea. It also gained control of Taiwan, the southern part of Sakhalin Island (north of Hokkaido), and Port Arthur, on the Chinese mainland.

The Japanese now turned increasingly on a course of empire-building. Siding with the Allied Powers in World War I, they saw little fighting. But the Allied victory brought them more territory in Manchuria, in northern China, as well as several Pacific Islands that had been held by Germany. Japan seized all of Manchuria in 1931 and set up a puppet government there under P'uyi, the last emperor of China, who had abdicated his throne in 1912. Manchuria provided Japan with new reserves of iron, steel, and coal. At the same time, militant nationalists gained control of the government, pushing the country on to greater expansion.

Japan invaded China in 1937 and quickly captured much of the eastern part of the country. After World War II broke out in Europe in 1939, the Japanese government formed an alliance with Germany and Italy and made plans for conquest in Southeast Asia and the Pacific. To prevent interference from the United States, Japanese forces staged the infamous December 7, 1941, surprise attack on American ships and bases at Pearl Harbor, Hawaii. This strategy worked only for a time. The attack brought the United States into the war, and while Japan extended its empire throughout much of Southeast Asia and the Pacific early on, the United States and its Allies ultimately rolled back those gains. The final blows came in August 1945, when the United States dropped atomic bombs on the Japanese cities of Hiroshima and Nagasaki. Emperor Hirohito announced Japan's surrender on August 14.

The war left Japan devastated and under Allied (chiefly U.S.) military occupation. Recognizing that a prosperous and democratic Japan would be less likely to invade its neighbors again, the occupying authorities focused on reviving the nation's economy and broadening participation in government. Under a new constitution, Japan forswore war. The emperor, no longer to be considered divine, was given only a ceremonial role in a government led by a prime minister and an elected legislature. Women were granted the vote. Large estates were broken up and the land given to farmers. The handful of families who controlled much of the country's industry (and had supported the war) were likewise required to break up their industrial empires.

Despite these and other sweeping changes, however, the occupiers avoided direct attacks on institutions and traditions that were central to Japanese culture. For example, many of Japan's wartime leaders were tried as war criminals before an international tribunal. But Emperor Hirohito was not charged, even though many people believed that he must have been complicit in actions for which others were tried.[1]

By the time Japan regained its independence in 1952, it was well on its way to prosperity. Heavy industries such as steel manufacturing were growing, and the government helped fuel the growth with subsidies, price controls, and protective regulations. In the years that followed, millions of Japanese left rural villages to take jobs in factories. A chain of cities spread along Japan's Pacific coast, and this metropolitan belt—*omote Nippon*, or "front Japan"—soon overshadowed the more rural west—*ura Nippon*, or "back-country Japan." Rapid economic growth brought prosperity to working families and laid the groundwork for a consumer revolution, as more and more people were able to afford cars, appliances, and other goods. Consumer demand in turn helped the economy grow still more. So did government-sponsored projects, including the development of fast "bullet" trains and other high-tech mass transit systems. But it was exports that drove the growth most strongly.

Japanese firms pursued foreign markets aggressively, pricing their products competitively. They also made sure that their products were in demand. They made quality a goal, so that the mark "Made in Japan"—once associated with cheap imitations of Western goods—became a sign of good workmanship and dependability. And they were quick to jump on the latest technological advances, especially in the field of electronics, and incorporate them into consumer products. For example, the first videocassette recorders were developed in the United States, but Japanese manufacturers were the first to produce affordable VCRs for home use, and they exported them all over the world. With successes like that, people began to talk about the Japanese economic "miracle"—and to wonder what it was about Japan that enabled the country to accomplish so much in so little time.

FAMILY AND COMMUNITY

Japan changed so radically in the twentieth century that a citizen of the Meiji Period would not know what to make of the country. Yet change didn't erase the cultural traditions that held Japanese society together, especially the high respect granted to the family. Today there are new pressures on these traditions, but they remain strong. Japanese children are still taught to put aside individual wants and needs for the good of the family—not just the nuclear family of parents and children but all the branches that make up the extended family, or house. Achievements are honored for the credit they bring to the house. Failure and wrongdoing bring shame on the house, and the person responsible will likely be shunned by other family members. In the traditional family hierarchy, youth defers to age, and women defer to men.

The family is the model for traditional Japanese communities, both rural villages and neighborhoods within major cities. Community associations made up of residents arrange everything from street repair to garbage collection. As in the family, individuals are expected to put the community's needs first. Consensus is important; those who disagree with the prevailing view are expected to go along. This sense of obligation to family and community is one reason why Japan traditionally has had a very low rate of violent crime. Now that the great majority of Japanese live in cities and are no longer surrounded by their extended families, family and community ties are no longer as strong as they once were, nor is the family hierarchy as strict. But the framework remains, and the attitudes it fosters are reflected throughout Japanese society, in business as well as personal relationships.

A worker—whether a factory hand or a corporate *sarariman*—is expected to be loyal to his employer and respectful to superiors. Confrontations are considered extremely poor manners, and frank negative opinions are rarely expressed. The success of the company, not the individual, is honored. Pressure to contribute to that success through overtime work and in other ways is intense. When Japanese businessmen work long hours and then go out with coworkers and business associates, drinking well into the night, they cement working relationships and establish trust. In fact, since sober people so rarely speak frankly in Japan, many Japanese believe they can't really get to know each other unless they drink together. Weekends may be taken up with corporate outings meant to further bond the group.

Women are generally excluded from these gatherings; Japanese women rarely hold important jobs, and wives aren't included in company functions. But with their husbands away from home so much of the time, wives are generally the chief decision makers when it comes to running the household and raising children.

The values of loyalty, harmony, and productivity fostered by these practices have been partly credited with the remarkable success of Japanese corporations, or *kaisha*, since World War II. In exchange for selfless devotion to their employers, workers in the postwar boom years gained affluence and the security of lifetime employment. But the blessings haven't been unmixed. Critics note that pressure to conform to the group and defer to superiors stifles innovation and creativity. Overtime and after-hours business functions aren't really voluntary—workers know they'll be ostracized if they don't take part. So, rather than the happy team members they sometimes seem to be, many Japanese workers are anxious and overworked, caught up in a web of duties and obligations that requires them to go along with the rest of their group.[2]

Japanese young people enter the world of work well-prepared for its pressures, thanks to values instilled by schools as well as families. The Japanese educational system was reorganized after World War II and is structured in much the same way as the U.S. educational system, with elementary schools, junior and senior high schools, and universities. Its students rank among the best in the world, at all levels. In early grades, the emphasis is on cooperation and responsibility. Students work together to set goals and solve problems, often debating the answers and correcting each other's mistakes. They cooperate to clean up classrooms and even serve lunch. Classes stay together through several grades, increasing the sense of community. Children who misbehave feel guilty for letting down the group, and that pressure is usually enough to stop the behavior. When teachers are absent, schools don't need substitutes—the students are able to get through the day on their own.[3]

After fifth grade, the emphasis shifts to academics. Young people know that their future success will depend on getting the right university education, and entrance to universities is based largely on entrance exams. They begin to drill for the exams early on, in school (six days a week, September through mid-July) and in after-school tutorial programs, focusing on memorizing facts—especially facts that are likely to turn up on exams. The level of academic achievement is high, but the system has been criticized for stifling initiative and creativity.

Young people are under tremendous pressure because failure to measure up in school will embarrass their families intolerably; indeed, failure has led some students to commit suicide. At the same time, the pressure to conform is strong—young people who stand out in any way are likely to be harassed by their peers. For example, Okano Yutaka, an English-language teacher in Osaka, notes that students study English grammar to pass university entrance exams but look askance at anyone who actually speaks it well.[4] At the same time, young people pepper their speech with adopted English words and phrases, often without knowing what the words mean. A 1997 *New York Times* story described high-school *gyaru* (gals), wearing fashionable *roozu sokusu* (loose socks), greeting each other by calling out *chekaraccho* (check it out, Joe).[5]

NEW SOCIAL PROBLEMS

Critics of the Japanese educational system worry that it produces students who have great knowledge at their fingertips but haven't really been trained to think, much less think creatively. They fear that these young people won't be prepared for the challenges of the next century. In the 1980s Japan seemed poised to help lead the world into the twenty-first century. But as the year 2000 drew closer, the Japanese found themselves dealing with a new set of problems at home.

The economy is no longer growing so rapidly; in fact, it has weakened. Prices on Japan's stock market were driven up by speculation in the 1980s; in the 1990s they dropped, wiping out a large part of many personal savings plans. At the same time, Japanese exports have faced growing competition abroad, from other Asian countries and from the United States. To encourage companies to become more efficient and competitive, the government has removed some of the price and distribution controls that had long cushioned Japanese businesses. As a result, companies now must pay more attention to profits and expenses, and some that once promised lifetime employment face the prospect of laying off workers. Many Japanese agree that reforms are needed—in politics and education as well as in business—to keep their country in a leading position. But they worry that the traditional ways of doing business, in which politeness, loyalty, and moral obligation are so important, will disappear as changes take hold.

Japan faces these changes with an aging population. It experienced a postwar "baby boom," as did the United States. Now people born then are growing older, while the birthrate has declined sharply. In 1997, for the first time, the number of Japanese over sixty-five exceeded the number of children under fifteen. In the current system, all workers get government-sponsored pension and health benefits from age sixty on, in addition to whatever pensions their employers provide. Providing these benefits for growing numbers of people may prove impossible, however. One projection showed that government pension reserves would run out by the year 2025 unless there were changes in the system, changes that would likely mean reduced benefits. But in a nation that traditionally respects and honors age, such changes are difficult.

Political corruption creates another set of difficulties for modern Japan. Through payoffs and favors, business leaders and party bosses have manipulated the government system for their personal gain. Corruption was at its worst in the 1970s and 1980s, when Kakuei Tanaka led the ruling Liberal Democratic party. Even after a 1974 bribery scandal forced Tanaka to step down as prime minister, he continued to control the party (and thus the government) from behind the scenes until 1989. Nor did corruption end with him; scandals have continued to surface, linking some of the country's highest officials to influence peddling. New leaders promise reform; but many Japanese have grown cynical about such promises, seeing only more of "the same old politics."[6]

Some of the corruption scandals have exposed links between business and organized crime—the Japanese mafia, or *yakuza*. Violent crime rates are still low in Japan, but organized crime operations are widespread. Established criminal organizations are quite open in some of their dealings, operating legitimate businesses as "fronts" sometimes even holding banquets for members. They control most of the thousands of enormously popular *pachinko* parlors, gambling halls where many hardworking Japanese lose a portion of their salaries every week, and have been implicated in blackmail and extortion schemes.

In cities such as Osaka and Tokyo, street gangs have also appeared, although they are not the problem that gangs are in the United States. The members are often young men who feel out of place in Japan's achievement-oriented society, perhaps because they have failed in school or have been unable to find work. Disaffected young people are also drawn to left- and right-wing extremist groups, some of which have been implicated in acts of terrorism. The number of people involved in gangs and extremist groups of all sorts is small—Japan is still a place where most people abide by social rules. But militant ultranationalist groups, which all but disappeared in the postwar years, have gained strength in the 1990s, a trend that many people find troubling. It was militant nationalism, after all, that embroiled Japan in World War II.

Memories of past wars color Japan's relations with other Pacific nations. North Korea, and South Korea in particular, distrust Japan because they have a long history of conflict. A chapter in that history is commemorated by the Ear Mound, a gruesome memorial in Kyoto. It marks the site where, four hundred years ago, Japanese soldiers buried more than 100,000 ears—cut from Koreans killed in a 1592 invasion, and brought back to Japan as proof of victory. More recently, after Japan annexed the Korean peninsula early in the twentieth century, thousands of Koreans were taken to Japan as forced laborers.

The Chinese likewise remember Japan's invasion of their country in the 1930s and the atrocities committed by Japanese troops then. And all the nations that fell to Japan in World War II, from Burma to the islands of the Central Pacific, were relieved when the treaty ending the war barred Japan from developing significant military forces. Since then, Japan's security has been guaranteed by the United States, which maintains bases on the Japanese island of Okinawa.

During the Cold War years, U.S. forces were seen as a bulwark against the spread of communism from China. There was an added benefit for Japan—freed from the expense of maintaining an army, it was able to put more of its resources toward economic development. Today, however, many Japanese resent the continued presence of foreign troops on their soil, and many Americans feel that maintaining the bases is an unnecessary expense. The U.S. government has urged Japan to take a greater role in its defense. But the arrangement isn't likely to change greatly in the near future, some analysts believe, because the U.S. troop presence helps deter conflict. It serves both countries and the region well, by helping to cool disputes that might lead to war.[7]

These days those disputes are more likely to involve trade than land. While Japan has some ongoing territorial squabbles with neighbors, economic influence is at the heart of international rivalry in the Pacific region. As its growth has slowed, Japan has seen countries such as Taiwan, Singapore, and South Korea blossom with their own economic miracles. At the same time, the Japanese have been pressured to end trade practices and subsidies that have given their exports an edge, and to dismantle the regulations that protect their own industries from domestic competition. The strongest pressure has come from the United States, which developed a huge trade deficit with Japan in the 1980s. While American consumers snapped up Japanese cars, televisions, and other products, U.S. companies complained that a maze of regulations kept their products off Japanese markets. Through trade agreements, the United States and Japan have taken steps toward solving this problem; but the complaint is still heard. In 1997 a trade war nearly erupted between the two nations over access to Japanese ports.

Some observers of Japanese-U.S. relations see these disputes as symptoms of deep differences in outlook. The United States has been among the world's strongest proponents of free trade and free markets, arguing that everyone benefits when products are allowed to compete on their merits without restrictions. In the past, Japan hasn't entirely embraced this view and has pursued whatever trade policy—free or protectionist—served its interest in a given situation.[8] The contrast has given rise to misunderstandings and resentment on both sides.

The events of 1997 brought new urgency to the debate over Japan's economic policies. Initially, Japan's currency and stock markets weathered the East Asian economic crisis well—having experienced sharp drops in value earlier in the decade, they weren't overvalued. But as a leading trading nation, Japan felt the effects of what happened elsewhere. As other East Asian economies staggered, the market for Japanese goods shrank. Unemployment and business bankruptcies, once virtually unheard of, became real worries. Loaded down with bad debts, banks stopped lending, putting more pressure on businesses and consumers.

The United States and other countries urged the Japanese government to take steps to revive the flagging economy—not only for Japan's sake, but for the entire region. If demand for imported goods increased in Japan, they reasoned, that would help everyone. In a culture where decisions are made by consensus, quick action proved difficult. But in April 1998 the Japanese government announced a $128 billion program of government spending, tax cuts, and other measures designed to put more money in the hands of Japanese consumers. Still, many people were doubtful that the incentives would work unless they were accompanied by an end to trade barriers and regulations that kept foreign goods from competing with Japanese products, sheltering Japanese businesses from foreign competition.

In parliamentary elections in July 1998, voters delivered a sharp rebuke to the ruling Liberal Democratic party for its handling of the economy. The party kept its majority, but it lost enough seats to prompt Prime Minister Ryutaro Hashimoto to resign. That threw the government's economic plans into confusion. As politicians argued over what to do next, the Japanese faced a deepening recession. A mounting number of banks and businesses teetered on the edge of collapse. Abroad, there was growing concern that Japan's hard times could spread worldwide.

3

CHINA
KEY TO THE RIM

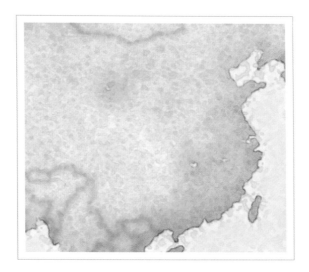

MOST OF CHINA'S MANY FARMING
COMMUNITIES ARE CONCENTRATED IN THE
RIVER VALLEYS. FARMERS IN CHINA'S
MOUNTAINOUS REGIONS CARVE TERRACES
INTO THE HILLSIDES TO GET MORE ACREAGE
FOR CROPS.

At newsstands in Beijing, shopping guides are among the top-selling items. Free of the political rhetoric that fills the gray columns of staid Chinese newspapers like the Communist party's *People's Daily*, these tabloid newspapers carry stories about movies, rock music, sports, fashion, and restaurants—along with page after page of colorful ads for clothes, furniture, computers, cosmetics, exercise machines, and scores of other consumer items. And for most readers, the ads are the draw. The types of consumer goods they showcase have been widely available only in recent years, and the ads are a way to learn about the latest products—even though many Chinese still can't afford to buy the items. Young people especially read the shopping guides to catch glimpses of the consumer-oriented, Western lifestyle that they aspire to. They want to dress in style, decorate their apartments, go out to dinner, see the latest films, hear the latest music.[1] In this, Beijing's young professionals are like their counterparts in cities all over the world. They differ in having less money to spend, but that doesn't keep them from dreaming.

But for many Chinese, such dreams seem pointless. For every young professional hunting for a bargain on a new CD player or a fashionable jacket, there are dozens of people hunting for ways to make ends meet. The situation is hardest in northeastern China, home to much of the country's heavy industry, where workers in huge state-run factories were once guaranteed security from cradle to grave. In the 1990s, in an effort to become profitable, factories there and throughout China began to cut millions of jobs. The result was the addition of a new phrase—*xia gang*, or "layoff"—and an unemployment rate that, in some cities, was estimated at more than 20 percent. The situation was no better in the countryside, where as many as 130 million people were without work.[2]

Because China's Communist system never envisioned high unemployment, there are few benefit programs in place to help those who suddenly lose their jobs. Some laid-off workers have continued to receive token payments, often less than $20 a month, from their former employers. Others have received nothing and have found themselves on the street, trying to earn a living as peddlers or day laborers. Even people who keep their jobs are hard pressed, since many industries have reduced wages. One result has been a growing number of labor demonstrations and protests, which authorities have done their best to squelch.

The contrasting lifestyles of young professionals and jobless workers are the result of changes that, beginning in the 1970s, have drawn this nation closer to the West. China steered a jagged course through the twentieth century, and it has yet to fulfill its enormous potential. That, by most accounts, is likely to change in the years ahead.

ASIA'S GIANT

China's sheer size makes it a major political and economic force in the Pacific Rim. With more than 1.2 billion people, it has the largest population of any country, and more than a fifth of the world's total population. In area, China is the world's third-largest country, spanning nearly 3,000 miles (4,800 kilometers) from the Russian border in the northeast to the Indian border in the southwest, in the high Himalayas. The varied land between is cut by great rivers that traditionally have been the country's lifelines, providing routes for trade and commerce as well as water for farming. The majority of China's people are farmers, but because much of China's land is too dry or mountainous for agriculture, the population is concentrated in the river valleys and other areas where good cropland is available. In many areas, farmers have carved terraces into the hillsides, to get more acreage for crops.

The Hwang Ho, or Yellow River, is the northernmost of the great rivers. It takes its name from the fact that its waters are often clouded with yellow soil washed from the mountains of the northwest. In the east, a broad river plain stretches out on each side of the Hwang Ho. This has long been one of China's most thickly populated regions, and the plain has been farmed for thousands of years. Several of China's most important cities, including Beijing, are north of the river, along with major industrial centers. Manchuria, in the northeast, is a source of iron and coal and a center for steelmaking.

The Yangtze takes a winding course through the heart of the country, emptying into the East China Sea at Shanghai, China's largest city. The Yangtze is the world's third-longest river and is so broad and deep along its lower reaches that oceangoing ships can travel up it nearly as far as Wuhan, about 500 miles (800 kilometers) from the coast. The region around the lower part of the river is one of the most crowded in China. Upriver, the Yangtze cuts through spectacular gorges and passes. It is the largest of four rivers that irrigate the sheltered Szechwan Basin in central China, one of the country's most important farming regions.

The Xi Jiang, South China's largest river, reaches the coast near Hong Kong. The South China coast is another thickly populated region, with a warm, moist climate that allows farming year-round. China produces a third of the world's rice, and this is China's greatest rice-growing region. Fishing boats and houseboats shelter in the many inlets and bays along the southern coast, and several major harbors handle ocean shipping.

The regions crossed by China's great rivers are the country's heartland and the birthplace of Chinese civilization—the world's oldest surviving civilization. Most of the people who live in northern, eastern, and southern China are Han Chinese, descendants of people who came into the area around the Hwang Ho about seven thousand years ago. As their numbers grew, they spread out into central and southern China. They took with them their language, culture, and a folk religion, based on ancestor worship and later incorporating Taoism and Buddhism. Cut off from the north by mountain ranges and rivers, Chinese communities in the southeast developed their own customs and several dialects that barely resemble Mandarin Chinese, the language spoken by more than half of China's people today. (One of those dialects, Cantonese, is the Chinese language most likely to be heard in North America, because many of the Chinese who have emigrated to America have come from the part of South China around Canton.)

China also expanded to include regions to the north and west, absorbing other cultures on the way. Several of these regions are still home to distinct ethnic groups with traditions and languages different from those of the Han Chinese. Mongol herdsmen ride the dry plains of Inner Mongolia. They share cultural roots with the people of Mongolia, just across the border. In medieval times, Mongols invaded China repeatedly and, under Kublai Khan and his successors, ruled it in the thirteenth and fourteenth centuries.

The Xinjiang-Uighur region, in the northwest, is a land of deserts, rugged mountains, and dry grasslands. Most of the people there trace their ancestry to Central Asia. The Uighurs are the largest group; others include Kazakhs, Kirghiz, and Uzbeks. They speak Turkic languages, like other Central Asian peoples, and many are Muslims. Although China has long controlled this region, few ethnic Chinese had much reason to live there until recent times, when large petroleum reserves were discovered.

Although the Chinese had made forays into Tibet in earlier times, they forcibly took control of this Himalayan nation in 1959. Traditionally, Tibetans followed a form of Buddhism known as Lamaism. Priests owned much of the land and had great power. With the Chinese takeover, the Dalai Lama and other leaders were forced to flee, and Lamaism was suppressed.

China has more than fifty other minority groups. Like the Tibetans, Mongols, and Uighurs, many of these groups have historically resisted the spread of Chinese culture into their areas. China's response has been to set up autonomous, or self-governing, regions for the largest groups, where they are free to follow their own ways, set up their own schools, and use their own languages. At the same time, the government has moved large numbers of ethnic Chinese into the most troublesome regions. In Inner Mongolia and Tibet, for example, ethnic Chinese now outnumber the natives, diluting the traditional culture and controlling public affairs.

ANCIENT WAYS, MODERN CONFLICTS

Traditional Chinese society was based on ideals laid out by the philosopher Confucius around 500 B.C. In this system, the family was at the center of daily life, and the father was the head of the family. Duty to parents, courtesy, and respect for elders were deeply held values. Women held a subordinate role, and marriages were often arranged to form strategic links between families. A typical household consisted of several generations living and working together—a man and his wife, their sons and the sons' wives and children, as well as any unmarried women in the family. Some households included as many as five generations, but many were smaller.

Poor farmers in particular could not afford to keep so many people under one roof, and sons often went off to form households of their own. Most farmers worked small plots, renting at least some of their fields from wealthy landowners. The landowners were an elite group, and some preferred to live in cities rather than in rural villages near their property. Cities were also home to laborers, shopkeepers, artisans, and merchants—everyone from the poorest to the wealthiest members of society. In the days of the Chinese empire, government officials were a unique group, scholarly civil servants who gained entry into their class by taking a set of examinations. In theory, anyone could become an official by taking the civil service exams, but in practice it was the wealthy classes that had the background, education, and time to prepare for and pass the tests.

This way of life, with its sharp contrasts between rich and poor, its strong traditions, and its regimented class structure, was dramatically reshaped in the twentieth century. A growing population, the development of industry, modern transportation and communication, and Western influence helped create pressure for change. By the early 1900s, Chinese intellectuals had come to believe that their country could never advance without sweeping political and economic reforms. The current emperor was a child, and the government was controlled by the Dowager Empress Tz'u Hsi (Cixi). She opposed change, and she was backed by powerful traditionalists. In 1911–1912 a revolution led by Sun Yat-sen overthrew the Manchu dynasty and set up a republic. The new government struggled to gain control as warlords formed their own armies and took control of large parts of the country. By 1926 Sun Yat-sen's successor, Chiang Kai-shek, had reunified the nation, but new threats emerged. Chinese Communists were stirring up rebellion, and in 1931 Japan invaded and seized Manchuria. Japan attacked again in 1937, starting eight years of war.

When World War II ended with Japan's defeat in 1945, China enjoyed only a few months of peace before fighting broke out between the Communists, led by Mao Zedong, and Chiang's Nationalists, or Kuomintang (KMT). The Communists had used the turmoil of the war years to good advantage, establishing a strong base in northern China and enrolling more than a million members. Now they moved south. After one of the biggest civil wars in modern history, the Nationalists were forced in 1949 to flee to the island of Taiwan, where they set up a separate government.

THE PEOPLE'S REPUBLIC

On the mainland, the Chinese Communist party (CCP) founded the People's Republic of China and set about restructuring society. Individuals could no longer own land; instead, the state took control and set up large farming communes. Party cadres, or activists, replaced landowners and civil servants as the new elite. Party-led work groups and community associations took over many of the roles once filled by extended families, such as caring for children and the elderly. New laws gave women greater independence, and new schools gave even poor children a chance for at least some education. Cities grew rapidly, as new industries brought people from rural areas to work in state-run factories.

These changes didn't come smoothly, nor did they bring all the benefits some hoped. Throughout the second half of the twentieth century, mainland China was torn repeatedly by power struggles between radicals, who wanted the country to stick to a strict Communist course, and moderates, who felt a more relaxed approach would speed economic growth. Although the Communists made progress in modernizing the country, China's standard of living lagged behind that of Western countries. And many Chinese chafed under the new regime. The government controlled most aspects of life, owning farms, businesses, and factories and determining where people lived and worked. Schools taught Communist theory and the ideas of Communist leader Mao Zedong. Political dissent was not allowed. Religion was suppressed. In an effort to keep the population from soaring out of control, couples were pressured to have no more than one child.

After Mao died in 1976, China slowly began to change. Under a new leader, Deng Xiaoping, the government began to allow free enterprise and private ownership of business. Deng's "market socialism" was welcomed both within China and abroad. The United States, which had refused to recognize the Communist government, finally established diplomatic relations with the People's Republic in 1979. Trade with the West increased. Especially in cities, Chinese business prospered, and U.S. and other foreign firms began to invest in China. This didn't happen all at once—power struggles within the government stalled progress several times. But by the early 1990s, China's economy was growing more than twice as fast as the economies of other developing nations.

While the changes brought new wealth to many people in China, they also brought problems. The gap between rich and poor once again widened. Overcrowding became a problem in the city as well as the countryside. With personal wealth once again allowed, corruption and bribery flowered. And since the late 1980s when the aging Deng began to withdraw from public life, the Chinese leadership has been torn by power struggles. When Deng died in 1997 at the age of ninety-two, no single person stepped in to take his place as China's most important leader. President Jiang Zemin and Prime Minister Li Peng, both veteran political survivors, contended with a tangle of factions within the CCP.

In 1998 Li was succeeded as prime minister by Zhu Rongji, who promised sweeping social changes. Zhu, a former mayor of Shanghai, had been head of economic policy since 1993 and had helped China break free from crippling inflation. And economic problems were high on the list that faced the new leaders.

TRADE AND ECONOMIC REFORM

When the 1997–1998 economic crisis swept Asia, China was among the least affected countries—largely because both its currency and large sectors of its economy are still under state control. But those same controls have stood in the way of growth, a fact that the country's leaders have become increasingly aware of.

One of the most important questions facing China today is what to do about inefficient state-run industries. Despite the growth of free enterprise since the 1970s, some 79,000 industrial companies were still under state control as of 1998, including 500 major manufacturing firms. Many were bankrupt, and Chinese banks were crippled by bad loans extended to keep them afloat. Corruption was rampant. When government dictates low prices for goods, but demand for those goods is high, it's tempting for factory managers to charge as much as people are willing to pay and then pocket the difference.

The government has gone after corrupt managers and officials, and it has stepped up an ambitious program of staff cuts, mergers, and management changes in the hope that many of these companies will be profitable and able to compete internationally early in the twenty-first century.[3] Some will be turned over to private control, and those that just can't turn a profit will be allowed to go bankrupt. The government is applying some of the same medicine to itself. In 1998 it announced plans to cut the number of government ministries from forty-one to twenty-nine and to reduce the number of government and Communist party employees by four million.

These steps are of great concern to government and factory workers, especially those in the targeted agencies and companies. At the same time, the government is abandoning some of the pillars of the old Communist system, such as subsidized housing. The subsidies have allowed workers, who typically make $100 a month, to live nearly rent free. How they will manage once rents are set by market forces—that is, the law of supply and demand—isn't clear.

What is clear is that China's fast-growing economy is producing wealth for some but poverty and unemployment for others. Finding jobs for the tens of millions of workers who have lost their jobs, and ensuring that social welfare programs continue in some form, is essential for the continued growth and stability of the country. China's leaders know that poverty breeds discontent and unrest. Even China's extraordinary economic growth rate—8 to 10 percent a year in the late 1990s—isn't enough to guarantee jobs for all. To keep that growth rate up, the government announced in 1998 that it would spend $1 trillion on public-works projects over the following three years. The most ambitious of those projects is the Three Gorges Dam on the Yangtze River.

Foreign trade and investment may help, but these activities are still tightly regulated. Western countries have long dreamed of getting a foothold in this vast market, and now, to a degree, they are getting a chance. But they often find that doing business in China is far from simple. To gain access to Chinese markets, foreign firms often must open plants in China and hire Chinese workers. Those that do quickly learn that patents are not always honored and trade secrets not always kept. For example, after the Du Pont company opened an agricultural chemicals plant in Shanghai in 1991, local businessmen stole the formula for a top-selling herbicide used in rice fields and started to produce and sell it on their own.[4] Du Pont had no recourse under Chinese law. However, even with that experience, the company has continued to do business in China. Many other U.S. companies have formed joint ventures with Chinese companies and opened factories there. The potential is just too great to pass up.

The restrictions China has placed on imports have hampered its ability to sell products abroad because other countries impose restrictions on Chinese products in return. China wants to join the World Trade Organization, a group of more than 120 nations that limits tariffs and other trade restrictions among members. To do so, it would have to lift many of its own restrictions on imports and stop subsidizing its industries. China would also like normal trade relations with the United States—that is, the same rights that most U.S. trading partners enjoy. But so far, such status has been awarded to China only temporarily. It has been renewed annually by Congress in a debate that focuses as much on China's record in human rights as on economic issues.

DEMOCRACY AND HUMAN RIGHTS

Many people have hoped that greater political freedom would follow China's new economic freedom. But that hasn't happened. The Chinese government has abandoned the economic underpinnings of communism; and privately, even party officials no longer support Communist ideals. But the party still controls the government, and the government is in firm control. Each time Chinese reformers have demanded greater democracy, the government has cracked down. Dissidents are routinely jailed, and free speech is suppressed. One of the most severe crackdowns took place in 1989, when the government used tanks and troops against thousands of student demonstrators in Tiananmen Square, in Beijing. The Tiananmen Square massacre prompted an international outcry and soured relations with Western nations.

The Chinese also dealt harshly with dissidents in Tibet, Xinjiang-Uighur, and other areas. Human-rights groups estimated that about three thousand political prisoners were being held in Chinese jails in the late 1990s, and many others were in labor and "re-education" camps. Beatings and torture are commonplace in the prisons and camps, according to numerous reports from survivors. Prisoners also provide a ready source of what amounts to slave labor. A dissident who served three years in a labor camp told of being put to work shredding rags by hand. She labored twelve hours a day in an unheated room, winter and summer.[5]

China has been widely condemned for repression by human-rights groups and by the United States and other democratic countries. Many human-rights activists believe that the United States should take a much stronger stand than it has. But the American policy has been to mute its criticism, to "engage" rather than alienate the Chinese, on the premise that a strong relationship is the best tool for making progress on human rights.

There has been some progress. The Chinese government has stopped trying to eliminate religious worship, although it still suppresses Lamaism, Christianity, and other faiths that it fears might become a focus for political unrest. A number of prominent dissidents have been released, generally at times when China has needed to look better abroad (for example, when the U.S. Congress is reviewing its trade status). And in October 1998 China signed the International Covenant on Civil and Political Rights, a United Nations (UN) treaty that guarantees freedom of expression, religion, assembly, and other basic rights.

In 1998 China permitted open elections for local offices. For the first time, voters in many towns and villages actually had a choice of candidates. But soon after he took office, Prime Minister Zhu made it clear that there would be no national elections anytime soon. "This process of direct elections is different in China than in foreign countries; it varies from the Orient to the Occident," he said.[6] That argument—that democracy is a Western institution that doesn't fit Asia—is one that has been used by other Asian leaders who hope to silence political opponents.

HONG KONG

China's tolerance for dissent is likely to be strongly tested in the territory of Hong Kong, which came under Chinese authority on July 1, 1997, after more than 150 years of British rule. Hong Kong's location on the South China coast has long made it a key Asian port. After World War II, millions of Chinese flooded into the territory to escape civil war and Communist rule in China. They helped make Hong Kong a lively center of world trade and finance, home to banks, manufacturers, and export firms. By 1996 well over six million people were living in the crowded territory.

For China, Hong Kong became a reminder of a bitter time—a colonial era when Western countries such as Britain dominated Asia. The Chinese made it clear that they would not renew Britain's lease when it ran out, and after difficult negotiations, China and Britain agreed in 1984 on a plan to return all of Hong Kong. China promised that Hong Kong would be a self-governing unit, able to keep its own economic system and way of life, for fifty years after the transfer.

Economic links between China and Hong Kong grew quickly. Many Hong Kong firms already had factories in southern China, and China soon became the largest investor in Hong Kong. Political unity was a different matter. Some Hong Kong residents looked forward to the end of British rule, but others had deep misgivings about the future and began to leave. In the years after the agreement was reached, Britain introduced a growing amount of democracy to the colony, including direct elections for its legislature. When the Chinese took control, they rejected these changes, disbanded the elected legislature, and installed a government composed largely of appointed officials. The new government quickly placed restrictions on political protests. Still, many of Hong Kong's people hoped for the best. Perhaps, they reasoned, officials in Beijing would come to see their thriving city as a model for the rest of China. And when Hong Kong's first election under Chinese rule was held in May 1998, voters turned out in force to elect a new legislature that included many of the ousted pro-democracy politicians.

CHINA AND THE PACIFIC RIM

The U.S. policy of building better relations with China was underscored in June 1998 when Bill Clinton became the first U.S. president to visit China since the 1989

Tiananmen Square massacre. Like the United States, most of the Pacific Rim nations recognize that China may hold the key to the future of the region. Its millions of people have a growing taste for consumer goods of all kinds, from electronics to clothing. If its economy continues to expand at anything like recent rates, more and more Chinese will be able to afford those products—and Pacific Rim nations are eager to supply them. Moreover, ethnic Chinese are a significant minority in many Pacific Rim nations, from Indonesia to the United States. Business and trade links are natural.

But if China is to fulfill its potential, it has much work to do. Although the Chinese government doesn't agree, many observers believe that greater freedom and democracy are essential for the country's stability. In addition, China has something of a rogue reputation in international relations. It is a major military power, with a large army and a cache of nuclear weapons, and its status as a nuclear power has caused concern. The Chinese continued to conduct underground nuclear tests into mid-1996, when other countries had voluntarily stopped such tests years earlier. And, violating international agreements, they have sold weapons and nuclear technology to other countries, including Iran and Pakistan, which tested a nuclear bomb in 1998.

China's military might has also made for uneasy relationships with neighboring nations, several of which have a history of conflict and/or long-simmering territorial disputes with China. The greatest potential for conflict lies just off the Chinese mainland—Taiwan, which still claims independence, and which China still claims as its own.

TAIWAN

IN THE SHADOW OF
THE MAINLAND

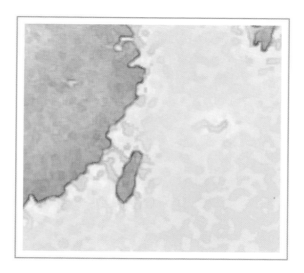

At Memorial Hall in Taipei, Taiwan, a larger-than-life statue of Chiang Kai-shek gazes over the hall and the public square beyond it. The figure is smiling—but if Chiang, who died in 1975, were still alive, he might not approve of what goes on in the square outside. It's a favorite site for political demonstrations—even protests against official government policy—that the Nationalist leader would never have allowed during his long years in power.

Ever since Nationalist forces under Chiang Kai-shek fled to Taiwan at the end of the Chinese civil war in 1949, Taipei has been the seat of government of the Republic of China (ROC). Taiwan has flourished during those years, becoming one of the most economically successful places in Asia. Yet the government of mainland China—the People's Republic—still regards Taiwan as a renegade province and insists that, one day, it will be under mainland rule. For its part, the Republic of China says it wants reunification with China—but only when the mainland enjoys the levels of democracy and prosperity found on Taiwan. So China and Taiwan watch each other carefully, facing off in what is, in effect, a long truce in the Chinese civil war.

MEMORIAL HALL IN TAIPEI IS DEDICATED TO CHIANG KAI-SHEK, LEADER OF THE NATIONALIST FORCES THAT FLED TO TAIWAN AFTER THE CHINESE CIVIL WAR IN 1949. TAIWAN HAS FLOURISHED AS THE REPUBLIC OF CHINA.

Taiwan was called *Ilha Formosa*, or "beautiful island," by early Portuguese explorers. Portugal was among several European countries that competed to set up trading bases on the island; in the 1600s the Dutch emerged as the winners in the competition. But in 1661 a Chinese pirate, Cheng Ch'eng-kung (or Coxingo), drove the Dutch out. Taiwan was absorbed into the Manchu empire by the end of the century, and many mainland Chinese settled there in the years that followed. At the end of the Sino-Japanese War in 1895, however, China was forced to cede Taiwan and nearby islands to Japan. Chinese residents on Taiwan rebelled, but the rebellion was crushed. For the next fifty years, Japanese rule was enforced harshly, and Japanese culture was imposed on the Taiwanese.

The islands were returned to China at the end of World War II, and Taiwan became a separate province. As fighting on the mainland increased, Nationalist soldiers and supporters arrived to secure the island for their side. Taiwan's residents found their new mainland governors high-handed and arrogant, and tension mounted. In February 1947 the situation exploded in an uprising that was quickly put down by mainland forces. Several thousand Taiwanese were killed. Today, some Taiwanese who were born on the island before the "mainlanders" arrived still resent them, especially since mainland Chinese have continued to dominate the government and, to a lesser extent, the economy. But that is fading as new generations grow up.

When Chiang Kai-shek and the remnants of his army arrived in 1949, his forces were already in firm control of Taiwan and several small island groups nearby. The Red Army was hot on Chiang's heels, but its plans to invade Taiwan were shelved when the United States sent ships to defend the island. Throughout the Cold War years, the need to protect Taiwan from the threat of Communist China was an unquestioned part of U.S. policy. The United States recognized the Republic of China as the true government of all China, signed a mutual defense treaty with Taiwan, and poured military and economic aid into the country. The aid, which continued into the mid-1960s, allowed Taiwan to start down the path of development that would turn it into an economic showcase. Traditional industries—farming and fishing—gave way to manufacturing as new factories turned out everything from electronic goods to toys and textiles.

Even as its economy boomed, however, Taiwan found itself increasingly isolated politically. More and more nations began to recognize the mainland government, and—since neither the People's Republic nor the Republic of China would admit the possibility of "two Chinas"—that meant breaking off formal diplomatic relations with Taiwan. In 1971 the People's Republic took over Taiwan's seat in the United Nations. When the United States finally recognized the People's Republic in 1979, it was one of the last countries to do so. But the United States kept up its commitment to defend Taiwan from military attack, and informal ties and trade links remained strong between Taiwan and countries around the world.

That has left Taiwan in an odd situation. Flourishing trade—especially with the United States, Hong Kong, and Japan—has made it one of the world's top-ranking exporters, an economic power by any standard. It has a strong army and acts in every way as an independent nation. Politically and diplomatically, however, it exists in a twilight zone, and it faces a constant threat of conflict with mainland China.

TAIWAN'S ECONOMY:
RIDING OUT THE STORM

Taiwan is one of the most densely populated regions anywhere, with more than 21.5 million people packed into less than 14,000 square miles (36,000 square kilometers), an area roughly the size of Connecticut and Massachusetts combined. Postwar prosperity has brought a good standard of living to the island; new cars cruise the highways, and Taipei boasts a state-of-the art subway system. When economic crisis swept through Asia in the late 1990s, Taiwan emerged in better shape than some of the region's nations. Several factors helped. First, Taiwan's exports have continued to grow, led by semiconductors, computer components, and other high-tech electronics products. The fact that exports outvalue imports gives Taiwan a healthy trade balance—it earns more selling goods abroad than it spends on foreign goods. It also has huge foreign-exchange reserves and comparatively little debt. Its banks are tightly regulated and take a conservative approach to lending; unlike banks in many Asian countries, they haven't taken on risky loans.

Taiwan is in this fortunate position thanks in part to lessons learned in the past. During the 1980s, real estate speculation ran wild and construction boomed. Office and apartment towers shot up everywhere. Speculators overbuilt, banks overlent—and in the early 1990s the bubble burst. Since then, Taiwan's business community has stayed focused on its strength, manufacturing. Electronics products, which accounted for just a small fraction of the island's output in the 1980s, now account for well over a third.[1]

Keeping up the sunny economic picture won't be easy. Taiwan manufacturers face competition from manufacturers in countries that, as a result of the Asian economic crisis, have devalued their currencies. This makes the competing products cheaper on world markets, forcing the Taiwanese manufacturers to cut their prices—and their profits. One way the Taiwanese see to stay ahead is through the development of new products. Especially in electronics, staying on top of new technology is essential.

EASING POLITICAL RESTRICTIONS

Perhaps most important, Taiwan needs political stability if it is to keep growing economically. In Chiang Kai-shek's day, that stability was enforced by strict, authoritarian rule. The Kuomintang, the party of the Nationalists, kept a firm grip on the government. Taiwan was under martial law from 1949 to 1987, which gave the government broad powers. Opposition groups were outlawed. The Nationalist view—which held that the Republic of China was the true government of all China—was the only view allowed.

Chiang Kai-shek served a total of five terms as president; on his death in 1975, he was followed by his vice president and then by his eldest son, Chiang Ching-kuo. When Chiang Ching-kuo died in 1988, vice president Lee Teng-hui took office—the first native of Taiwan to serve as president.

Lee, who was elected to a full six-year term in 1990, carried out a process of liberalization that began with the lifting of martial law. Opposition political parties were allowed to take part in general elections for the first time, and open parliamentary elections were held in 1992. Among the new parties was the Democratic Progressive party, which openly advocated independence for Taiwan. In Chiang's day, people would have been jailed for even suggesting that Taiwan might go its own way without the rest of China. At the other end of the political spectrum were those who supported the mainland government's claims to Taiwan. Just a few years earlier, that would have been treason.

Taiwan also began informal negotiations with China, seeking ways to ease tensions. The Nationalist government renounced the use of force against the mainland in 1991, and it began to permit its citizens to travel there. Many people in Taiwan have family members on the mainland, and in recent years economic ties have grown as well. It has become commonplace for Taiwanese to visit their ancestral homes on the mainland and visit old friends and relatives. Chinese on Taiwan and the mainland also began to do more business; by the mid-1990s, Taiwan companies had invested some $20 billion in facilities on the mainland, where labor costs were considerably lower.[2]

A CONFRONTATION, BUT NO SOLUTION

By 1995 China and Taiwan were on the verge of starting direct air service and opening ports to each other's ships. But then tension flared, after China made a formal proposal for reunification. It called for "one country, two systems"—that is, Taiwan would be governed by Beijing but allowed to keep its own way of life, like Hong Kong. Lee rejected the plan, saying reunification under a Communist dictatorship was impossible. He repeated Taiwan's position—that reunification should come only after China introduced democracy and raised its standard of living to a level closer to that of Taiwan. And he denounced China for refusing to follow Taiwan's lead and give up the threat of using force to settle the issue.

Lee also began to press for Taiwan to have its own seat in the United Nations, offering to give $1 billion to the United Nations if Taiwan could be admitted as a member. The offer was turned down; all the same, it incensed the mainland government, which saw it as an attempt to win recognition for "two Chinas." Then, in June 1995, Lee became the first leader of Taiwan to visit the United States. The visit was unofficial—he went to deliver a speech at Cornell University, where he had attended college—but it infuriated China, which saw it as another part of a master plan to gain international recognition for an independent Taiwan. In fact, when President Bill Clinton gave Lee permission to visit the United States, China accused the U.S. administration of encouraging a Taiwanese bid for independence.

Many observers thought that Lee was probably less interested in independence than in gaining support in Taiwan's first free presidential election, set for March 23, 1996. Although he officially adhered to the Nationalist party goal of eventual reunification, he needed to court pro-independence voters to win at the ballot box. But to Chinese officials, the vote itself seemed to be a step toward Taiwanese independence. Two weeks before the election, in a step that was clearly intended to intimidate Taiwanese voters, they began a series of missile tests in the ocean right off Taiwan. Some of the tests were less than 25 miles (40 kilometers) off the island's southeastern coast, near busy shipping lanes. The action prompted the United States to send two aircraft carrier battle groups to the region, as a warning to China.

In the end, China's scare tactics backfired. Voters turned out in force and chose Lee by more than two to one over any of his three opponents. After the vote, both sides stepped back from the confrontation. Taiwan turned its focus back to its economy, and talk of independence died down. China also toned down its rhetoric, and the situation settled back into an uneasy, watchful truce.

The 1996 confrontation did nothing to solve the underlying question of Taiwan's status. Taiwan's leaders are not likely to agree to rejoin China under its current government. And Taiwan—unlike Hong Kong, which faced the deadline of an expiring lease and so had to come to terms with China—is under no great pressure to solve the problem. On the other hand, China's leaders view Taiwan's status as a matter of national pride and sovereignty: They consider it a province and Lee a provincial leader, and they are not likely to change that view. As long as that is the case, the potential for future conflict remains. Such a conflict, if it comes, would send shock waves throughout the Pacific.

THE KOREAS

TENSIONS AT THE BORDER

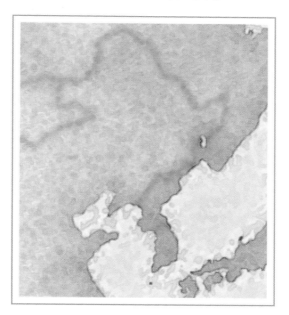

THE FORTIFIED BORDER THAT DIVIDES NORTH KOREA AND SOUTH KOREA SLICES THROUGH A LAND OF GREAT NATURAL BEAUTY. SOUTH KOREA HAS DEVELOPED ECONOMICALLY MORE RAPIDLY THAN NORTH KOREA, LEADING MANY IN THE SOUTH TO QUESTION THE VALUE OF REUNITING WITH THE NORTH.

A double row of barbed wire stretches across the middle of the Korean peninsula. On one side is the People's Democratic Republic of Korea—North Korea, one of the world's last and most extreme Communist countries. On the other is the Republic of Korea—South Korea, which has amazed the world with its economic growth. The border between them is one of the most heavily fortified places on earth. On either side, soldiers—1.5 million in all—face off against each other, ready at a moment's notice to fight. It's also one of the world's weirdest tourist attractions. At points along both sides of the border, buses pull up and disgorge curious visitors who stare at the other side through binoculars. A Korean man on the northern side of the border watches soldiers patrol on the south side and muses, "They could be my relatives."[1]

The fortified border that slices through Korea is a legacy of bitter war. The peninsula was divided after World War II as a result of the growing rivalry between Communist nations, led by the Soviet Union, and capitalist countries, led by the United Sates. In 1950, Korea became one of the few places where the Cold War turned hot. Fighting between North and South Korea ended in a truce in 1953, but there was no formal peace agreement. Thus the barbed wire, the soldiers—and the risk of renewed war—remain.

THE HERMIT KINGDOM

A mountainous land of spectacular natural beauty, the Korean peninsula juts out from the Chinese coast toward Japan. The Koreans are descendants of people who came to this land from Central Asia thousands of years ago. Even today, there are no sizable minority groups. As the Kingdom of Choson, ruled by the Yi dynasty for five hundred years, Korea managed to fend off repeated invasions by Japan and China. It also closed its doors to the West, banning missionaries and merchants alike.

Thanks to its isolation, Korea became known as the Hermit Kingdom.

By the late 1800s, however, the kingdom was weakened by a series of famines, rebellions, and factional disputes. It became a pawn in mounting rivalry between Japan and Russia. Japanese troops swept through the Korean peninsula in 1905 at the start of war with Russia, and after Russia's surrender, Korea had no protector against Japan's colonial ambitions. Japan governed what had been the independent kingdom of Korea as a protectorate, taking over foreign and military affairs and disbanding the Korean army. In 1910, Japan fully annexed Korea.

The Japanese began to modernize Korea's economy, but few Koreans profited because industry and government were organized to benefit Japan. The Japanese also tried to wipe out Korean culture, even banning the Korean language. Protests were brutally crushed. Some Koreans formed anti-Japanese guerrilla groups; many left for Manchuria and Siberia. Korean independence groups formed a government-in-exile and chose Syngman Rhee, a teacher and Christian missionary who had been educated in the United States, to lead it. But he could not hold the groups together, and before long they had split up into pro-Communist and anti-Communist factions.

During World War II, Syngman Rhee pressed his country's case in Washington, D.C., and won a commitment from the United States and its allies to back Korean independence. But when the war ended, the old factional disputes remained—and they were made worse by the fact that the Soviet Union threw its weight behind the pro-Communist groups, while the United States backed anti-Communist groups. The Soviets occupied Korea north of the 38th parallel of latitude, and the United States south of that line. Each quickly went about molding its zone into a future ally. The result for Korea was disastrous—by 1948, the peninsula was divided between Communist North Korea, backed by the Soviet Union, and capitalist South Korea, supported by the United States.

In the North, Kim Il Sung, a former Soviet soldier and the Communist party leader, established his capital at Pyongyang and began to build a socialist state. The North also built an army, and in June 1950 it sent that army over the 38th parallel into South Korea, in a bid to control the entire peninsula. North Korea had the military support of the Soviet Union and China. But South Korea had the United Nations Command—a force made up of troops from sixteen nations, led and dominated by the United States. After three years of fighting that left more than a million people dead, the war ended with a truce. The peninsula was still divided.

IN THE SOUTH

South Korea made a start toward democracy, under a constitution that created a republic. But Syngman Rhee, the first president, engineered a number of constitutional changes that allowed him to hang on to power. South Koreans grew increasingly dissatisfied with Rhee's control, and opposition groups formed to challenge him. The dissatisfaction came to a head in 1960, when a violent student uprising toppled his government. Once again, democracy tried to take root. But in 1961 a bloodless coup put Major General Park Chung Hee in control.

Park, more than anyone, put the country on the path to rapid industrialization. He had been educated in Japan and was a great admirer of Japan's postwar economic success, which he now set out to duplicate. Steelmaking, shipbuilding, electronics, and other "strategic" industries were carefully nurtured and subsidized by the government. Foreign competition was kept out. Workers put in twelve-hour days, six days a week; some even slept at work. Those who didn't could be fired. Those who protested could be jailed.

The result was phenomenal growth. In a generation, South Korea went from a war-torn, undeveloped nation to one of the world's leading exporters of manufactured goods. Seoul, the capital, became a city of modern skyscrapers. But democracy was not part of Park's plan for the country, and his rule was autocratic. His refusal to allow reforms eventually led to his assassination, by his own security chief, in 1979.

After Park's death, martial law was declared, and Major General Chun Doo Hwan seized power. In May 1980, Chun sent troops to the southwest city of Kwangju to crush a revolt. At least 148 people were killed, and about 1,700 were arrested. The Kwangju massacre, as the incident was called, became a rallying point for the opposition. In 1987 when Chun tried to install another general, Roh Tae Woo, as his successor, a wave of student-led protests swept the country. Roh announced that he would seek office through a popular vote. He managed to win the presidency with just 37 percent of the vote; opposition parties split the rest. Five years later, the country's first civilian president, Kim Young Sam, was elected as a coalition candidate. He led an anticorruption campaign that put Roh and Chun on trial for bribery and, separately, mutiny and treason for their roles in the 1979 coup and 1980 Kwangju massacre. Chun's sentence was death, later commuted to life in jail; Roh's, more than twenty-two years in prison. (Both were pardoned in December 1997.)

NEW FREEDOMS, NEW PROBLEMS

By the mid-1990s, South Koreans enjoyed greater democracy, better pay, and shorter working hours than they had in the past. Their industries, guided and protected by the government, had grown into huge conglomerates. But there were problems with the breathtaking success story. South Korea's banks and businesses had borrowed huge amounts from foreign investors to fund expansion and construction. When the Asian financial crisis began in 1997, investors lost confidence in South Korea's ability to repay those debts. Stock prices fell by a third, and the value of South Korean currency was nearly cut in half. In November 1997 South Korea was forced to turn to the International Monetary Fund (IMF) for a $57 billion rescue package. In exchange for guaranteed loans to help the country pay off its debt, the IMF won promises from South Korean leaders to ease restrictions on foreign ownership of business, lift most barriers to imports, and end subsidies to ailing companies.

Korean voters were dismayed to see their hard-won prosperity slipping away. In December 1997 they showed their disapproval of the government by electing a new president: Kim Dae Jung, a veteran opposition leader. He had been jailed, and at one point even sentenced to death, for opposing South Korea's military rulers in the 1980s. Now he promised democracy, free markets, and social justice.

Kim Dae Jung's chances of success—and his country's future—hinge on two factors. One is its ability to recover from its financial crisis. The second is its relationship to North Korea.

LIFE IN THE NORTH

When South Koreans look across the demilitarized zone that separates them from the North, they see a country that is isolated, poor, and ruled by an oppressive and secretive government. North Korea began as a Marxist-Leninist state, modeled on the Soviet Union. But under

Kim Il Sung, it soon became a totalitarian dictatorship in which the leader's every word was law, and his government sought to control every aspect of life. After the death of Kim Il Sung in July 1994, his son Kim Jong Il stepped into the leadership role.

Kim Il Sung promoted a homegrown version of communism called *Juche* (or self-reliance) ideology. This philosophy views the nation as a sort of living being in which the supreme leader is the brain, and the masses are required to obey his dictates without question. The North Korean constitution guarantees freedom of speech, press, and assembly, but in practice the people have none of these rights. The leader's authority is absolute, and citizens are expected to be unswervingly loyal in carrying out each of his instructions.

Power is in the hands of the Communist party, the Workers' Party of Korea. There are other political parties—but they are controlled by the Workers' Party. The official line is that political parties must not compete for power: "True democracy can be guaranteed only when the centralized guidance of the government can be practiced under the leadership of the working-class party."[2] There's a legislature, too; but it exists only to rubber-stamp policies set by the party leadership, and it has never rejected a bill proposed by the government. In elections for the assembly, voters are presented with one candidate for each district—guaranteeing 100 percent support for the Workers' Party. The president's powers are defined so loosely in the constitution that they are practically limitless.

To outsiders, life in North Korea sounds like something from the pages of *1984*, George Orwell's novel about life under a totalitarian government. Visitors to Pyongyang describe silent streets and parks that are eerily empty, as if people were afraid to use them.[3] Beginning in the 1960s, the government sorted all citizens into three classes: the "core class," made up of party members and loyalists; the "unstable class," mainly ordinary workers; and the "hostile class," which includes families of defectors and anyone considered a dissident. The State Security Agency monitors everyone, using spies, informers, and electronic eavesdropping, to make sure they toe the party line. Backing up the secret police is something called the five-household system, in which households are organized into teams. A party worker supervises the households in self-criticism sessions and other ideological activities, and all the residents are encouraged to inform against each other.

Religion is suppressed, and travel outside the country is out of the question for most North Koreans. Even travel within the country is restricted. North Koreans are required to apply for a travel permit to go from one part of the country to another. This rule is not always enforced today, and there have been signs that the younger Kim may relax some other state controls. For the most part, however, life in North Korea hasn't improved under the new leader.

In fact, from an economic standpoint, it has gotten worse. Aid from the Soviet Union and China helped North Korea recover from the Korean War. But that aid began to decline in the 1960s. The collapse of the Soviet Union in 1991 was a devastating blow—not only did it end hopes of aid, it eliminated North Korea's main trading partner. North Korea's state-run industries aren't competitive abroad, and its collective farms don't produce enough food to make the country self-sufficient. In the late 1990s, when floods followed by drought compounded their troubles, North Koreans faced severe famine. The government was forced to appeal to the world for food aid, something that had never happened before.

To get out of this quagmire, many observers say, North Korea will have to follow the route taken by the former Communist states of Eastern Europe—allowing free-market reforms and opening its borders to foreign trade. It's still not clear whether Kim Jung Il will be able to shake off the ideology and government systems he inherited. However, the country has made a few efforts to court foreign investors, creating a free-trade zone and passing a law permitting joint business ventures. It has also made overtures to Japan and increased economic contacts with the South. South Korean industries want to establish joint ventures in the North, where labor is cheap, and import cheap goods from the North. For this trade to take place, North and South Koreans turn to other countries, who act as intermediaries between them.

NORTH-SOUTH RELATIONS

From the start, the stated goal of both North and South Korea has been to unify the peninsula—but each wants to be the one whose system prevails. The relationship between South and North has changed over the years, but the level of mistrust between them remains high. Both have poured billions of dollars into maintaining their armies. South Korea still has its alliance with the United States as a shield, and about 37,000 American troops are still stationed there.

In the late 1980s and early 1990s, the collapse of communism in Eastern Europe ended the highly charged Cold War atmosphere that separated North and South. South Korea began to build ties with former Communist states, and North Korea found itself increasingly isolated on the world scene. In December 1991 the South and the

North signed a historic agreement that was designed to ease tensions and increase exchanges and economic cooperation. But the agreement wasn't carried out, and tensions between North and South remained high—the more so with mounting evidence that North Korea was trying to develop nuclear weapons. In 1994 the United States got North Korea to agree to international inspections of its nuclear facilities, in exchange for help in developing nuclear power plants that would have no capability to produce weapons. But there were indications that the North Koreans simply moved their weapons program to secret locations.

In 1997 North Korea agreed to take part in four-way negotiations with South Korea, the United States, and China. Even before he took office in 1998, Kim Dae Jung called for broader exchanges with the North. But there has been little progress toward the goal of permanent peace. Many South Koreans are no longer in a rush to reunify the peninsula—that would mean taking on the vast problems of the poverty-stricken North while they were facing their own set of economic troubles. And with the North Koreans repeatedly threatening to renege on the truce that ended the Korean War, tensions have remained high.

6

MAINLAND SOUTHEAST ASIA

A TROUBLED PAST

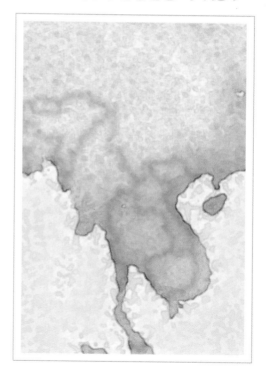

In the fall of 1997 a parking garage in downtown Bangkok, Thailand, became host to a weekend flea market with some unusual goods. On the block were secondhand designer clothes, Mercedes-Benz cars, expensive watches and jewelry—all the trappings of wealth, including a private airplane. The sellers were Thailand's "formerly rich"—people who had lost money when the country's fast-growing economy took a sharp downturn in the middle of the year. Now they were selling many of their prized possessions to make ends meet.[1] The status-symbol sale might have been amusing if it weren't for the rest of the story: For every wealthy person hit hard by the downturn, there were scores of laid-off factory workers and others who were so poor that they had nothing to sell.

Thailand's 1997 troubles triggered a wave of doubt that led to similar downturns in other countries, and by year-end Southeast Asia was gripped by a serious economic crisis. The result was an end to many dreams and to the hope that seemingly endless growth would bring a better life for all. But few people thought that the problems would be more than a temporary setback. Southeast Asia has bounced back from adversity many times.

THE GREAT RICE-PRODUCING REGION OF SOUTHEAST ASIA IS DOTTED WITH SMALL VILLAGES SUCH AS THIS ONE IN THE RUGGED MOUNTAINS OF VIETNAM. THE RICE PADDIES IN THE FOREGROUND PROVIDE A LIVING FOR THE VILLAGERS.

The peninsula that forms mainland Southeast Asia juts out from the Chinese coast into the South China Sea. It's a varied and beautiful land, with rugged mountains, thick tropical forests, and flat river valleys where farmers have carved out rice paddies from every possible square foot of land. This has long been one of Asia's great rice-producing regions, and it might produce even more were it not for a troubled and violent past.

Southeast Asia's history is marked by rivalries between its nations and periods of domination by outsiders—first the Chinese, whose culture had a deep impact on the region, and then the Europeans. France ruled much of the peninsula for eighty years, until the 1950s. Then, in the 1960s and 1970s, the region became a battleground in the struggle between Communist and non-Communist nations. In many ways, the countries of mainland Southeast Asia are still struggling with the legacy of their years of conflict. This chapter will visit three of those countries: Vietnam, Cambodia, and Thailand.

VIETNAM

Vietnam lies along the eastern edge of the peninsula, with a long coastline on the South China Sea. For more than a thousand years, beginning in 111 B.C., China controlled the mountainous northern part of this country. The Vietnamese were able to shake off Chinese rule only for brief periods until A.D. 939, when they finally won independence. Over the centuries that followed, the Vietnamese in the north gradually extended their kingdom down the coast to the flat, steamy Mekong River delta.

Nine hundred years of independence came to an end in the mid-1800s, when the French arrived. Determined to build an empire, the French gained control of Vietnam piecemeal. By the 1880s they had most of it, and in

1899 Vietnam was combined with neighboring Laos and Cambodia as the colony of French Indochina. The French had high ideals as colonial rulers—they spoke of their mission to bring the benefits of European civilization to this region. But the Vietnamese, who had a highly developed civilization of their own, were less enthusiastic. Resistance to French rule grew, and by the 1920s a nationalist movement was gathering strength. Among its leaders was Nguyen Tat Thanh, who later took the name Ho Chi Minh and founded the Indochinese Communist party.

Ho and other nationalists fought Japanese occupation during World War II. After the war, Ho established the Democratic Republic of Vietnam in the north, with Hanoi as the capital. But the French were not ready to give up their colony, and they tried to keep control in the south. After eight years of fighting, the French withdrew under a 1954 peace agreement that split the country along the 17th parallel. Ho kept control in the north, establishing a Communist dictatorship. The government of the South, facing a threat from Communist guerrillas, turned to the United States for aid. Like Korea, Vietnam became a Cold War hot spot. From the mid-1960s on, the United States was drawn deeper into the conflict that became known as the Vietnam War. The war became extremely controversial in the United States, and some 58,000 American soldiers died before the United States withdrew its combat forces under an agreement signed in 1973. By the time the war ended with the victory of North Vietnamese and Communist guerrilla forces in 1975, more than a million Vietnamese had died.

Years of fighting had devastated the country's economy, and the situation wasn't helped when the Communist government set about imposing controls on the

South. Political freedom was sharply curtailed, and thousands of people were sent to "re-education centers" that were essentially labor camps in remote jungle areas. Private trade was banned, farms were reorganized as government-owned collectives, and the government took over many businesses. The Vietnamese call what followed "the ten bad years"—because of the hardships created by government policies, theirs became one of the world's poorest countries.[2] Ethnic Chinese, who traditionally had been shopkeepers and businesspeople, were especially hard hit. Many had no way to earn a living. They made up a large portion of a growing stream of refugees— "boat people"—who fled the country in search of freedom and opportunity.

The "ten bad years" ended after Vietnam's leaders, like Communist leaders elsewhere in the late 1980s, admitted the need for at least some private enterprise. It would have been especially hard for Vietnam to ignore the need—Asian Pacific nations all around it were rolling in new wealth. In 1989 Vietnam opened its doors to foreign investment, and five years later the United States lifted the trade embargo it had imposed on its former enemy in 1975. In 1995 formal diplomatic relations were restored between the United States and Vietnam, and Vietnam became the first Communist member of the Association of South East Asian Nations (ASEAN), an economic and trade association that has played an important role in the region's growth.

With investment pouring in, new hotels and office towers have sprung up in Hanoi and Ho Chi Minh City (formerly Saigon). Developers have staked out sites for resorts along the coast. So far Vietnam's transformation has been far from complete, however. The government still keeps a leash on business, and investors know that they'll have to pay many bribes to get the approvals they need for their projects. In the countryside, where most Vietnamese live, poverty is the rule, and many children suffer from malnutrition. Political freedom is still limited, although the controls are not as tight as they once were. But even with these problems, the changes in Vietnam have encouraged some of the refugees who fled in the 1970s to return to their homeland.

CAMBODIA

While Vietnam is finally starting on the road back from the devastation caused by war, Cambodia is still struggling to free itself from civil conflicts. The hardships endured by the Vietnamese pale beside those of the Cambodians, who lived a nightmare in the 1970s and have been dealing with its consequences ever since.

Vietnam and Cambodia are ancient rivals that, nevertheless, have much in common. The heart of Cambodia is a broad lowland, ringed by mountains and crossed by the Mekong River. In ancient times this fertile rice-growing region was the center of the Khmer empire, which by the 1300s controlled a large part of Southeast Asia. But rebellions and invasions, from Vietnam to the east and Thailand to the west, chipped away at the empire, and in the 1800s what remained of it—the kingdom of Cambodia—became a French protectorate and then a part of French Indochina.

Norodom Sihanouk, who became king in 1941 at the age of eighteen, led the movement that gained independence for Cambodia in 1953. Sihanouk resigned the monarchy, which was mostly ceremonial, in 1955 so that he could play an active role in government. As fighting between Communist and non-Communist forces in neighboring Vietnam grew, he tried to keep Cambodia neutral. That proved impossible. He was pressured on one side by the Khmer Rouge, a Cambodian Communist group, and on the other by the United States and other opponents of communism. In 1970 he was overthrown by General Lon Nol, a staunch anti-Communist. Five years of civil war between the government and the Khmer Rouge followed—and the Khmer Rouge emerged victorious in 1975.

The Khmer Rouge established one of the most brutal regimes in modern history. Thousands of people were forced to leave the capital, Phnom Penh, and other cities to work on new collective farms in the countryside. Education and technology were all but eliminated under the bizarre programs outlined by the Khmer Rouge leader, Pol Pot. Families were separated, and private property was abolished. More than one million people died—many shot by the Khmer Rouge for such "crimes" as having an education, many from starvation and disease that were a result of Khmer Rouge actions.

The Khmer Rouge was driven from power in 1979 by an invading force from Vietnam. The Vietnamese established control over most of Cambodia's cities and set up a puppet government in Phnom Penh, the capital. But the Khmer Rouge held large sections of the countryside, and they continued to fight a guerrilla war against the new government even after Vietnamese troops withdrew. Eventually several other factions, including a group loyal to Norodom Sihanouk, joined the fight.

In 1991 the warring factions finally agreed to a UN peace plan. Two years later elections were held. The Khmer Rouge boycotted the vote, and parties led by Sihanouk and his son, Norodom Ranariddh, won the most votes. But Hun Sen, leader of what had been the Communist party in the days of Vietnamese control, would not accept the results unless he was named joint prime minister with Ranariddh. That proved to be a disaster. Far from sharing power, the two prime ministers rarely consulted and even maintained separate military forces. In 1997, after Ranariddh tried to open negotiations with the Khmer Rouge, Hun Sen staged a coup and drove him from the country. Hun Sen held onto power in a July 1998 election that was widely criticized as rigged, but Ranariddh was allowed to return as leader of an opposition group.

The Khmer Rouge was also torn by divisions. Many of its members had grown sick of life in the malaria-infested forests and longed for peace. Pol Pot tried to crush a splinter movement by killing its leaders in 1996, but in the end he was captured by his rivals. They staged a show trial and sentenced him to life imprisonment—ironically, for the 1996 murders, not for the million-plus deaths he had caused as Cambodia's ruler in the 1970s. No one outside the Khmer Rouge recognized this trial as justice, and the United States led an international effort to bring Pol Pot before an international tribunal. But Pol Pot died in April 1998, before that could happen. The seventy-three-year-old leader was said to have died in his sleep, of natural causes, and his body was quickly cremated. But there were lingering suspicions that he had been killed by his comrades.

Although government forces were closing in on the remnants of the Khmer Rouge, no one expected Cambodia's troubles to end with the death of Pol Pot. The years of Khmer Rouge rule had destroyed the country's business and professional classes, along with its educational system. The years of fighting that followed had scared off foreign investors and kept the country from recovering. And politically, Cambodians remained deeply divided. It would take many years to fix the damage that had been done.

THAILAND

Alone among Southeast Asian nations, Thailand was never a European colony; nor was it a battleground in the conflicts that swept the region in the 1960s and 1970s. As the Kingdom of Siam, beginning in the 1200s, the country was ruled by absolute monarchs who gradually expanded their territory until, by the 1800s, they headed the most powerful state on the peninsula.

When European powers began to build colonial empires in the region, Siam lost some territory but not its independence. Nevertheless, Europeans had a significant impact on the country from the 1850s on. With the help of European advisers, Thai kings revised the educational system along Western lines, built modern transportation systems, abolished slavery, and developed a modern army. After a bloodless coup in 1932, Thai kings took a figurehead role. Thailand became a constitutional monarchy; however, for much of the time since then, true power has rested with a series of military leaders. They kept a Communist insurgency in check through the 1970s and began an ambitious program of economic development.

Thailand remains one of the world's leading rice producers. But in the 1980s, Japan and other nations sought cheap labor for industries, and they found it in Thailand, where the population includes ethnic Thais, Chinese, and Malays, as well as Vietnamese and Cambodians who arrived as refugees from recent conflicts in Southeast Asia. Many Thai citizens crowded into Bangkok and other cities, to find work in expanding garment factories and other industries. For a decade, there were plenty of jobs—but the pay was low, and workers often had to support not only themselves but extended families still living in rural villages. Thailand's economic boom produced extraordinary wealth for a few people but little for average workers. In fact, the gap in income between the country's rich and poor was one of the five widest in the world, according to the World Bank.[3]

Thailand also borrowed heavily abroad, and its lax regulations allowed banks to finance all sorts of uncreditworthy projects. By 1997 the country was awash in half-empty office and apartment buildings and unprofitable shopping centers, built on speculation with borrowed funds. Banks that had financed the construction boom were left holding bad loans. The Thai stock market headed down. Currency traders sensed that the Thai economy was overextended and began to sell off their holdings of the Thai currency, the baht. At first, the Thai government tried to support the baht—that is, keep its value up by buying it on international markets, using government reserves of foreign currency to do so. But it was finally forced to devalue the baht. That was a disaster for foreign lenders and investors, who saw the value of their holdings plummet. More and more Thai businesses closed their doors, putting two million workers on the streets.

In the fall of 1997 a new prime minister, Chuan Leekpai, took office. He undertook sweeping reforms that would allow Thailand to qualify for $17 billion in loans and guarantees from the International Monetary Fund (IMF). The country also adopted a new constitution— one that guarantees press freedom, mandates universal education through twelfth grade (rather than sixth), and holds government leaders to higher standards of accountability. The constitution had been in the works for years, but had been blocked by conservative politicians until the economic crisis underlined the need for change.

If the reforms take hold, many observers think, Thailand and other nations of Southeast Asia may emerge from the downturn stronger than ever. That will be good news for their Pacific trading partners, including the United States. Because of the U.S. role in the fighting that engulfed Vietnam, Cambodia, and Laos in the 1960s and 1970s, this part of Southeast Asia has special significance for Americans. The end of the Cold War and the collapse of international communism in 1989–1991 changed, but did not end, the region's importance. From a U.S. point of view, democracy and free-market systems will make Southeast Asian nations strong trading partners and allies—and good counterweights against expanding Chinese influence. That is why the United States and other Western nations have strongly supported the IMF's programs to help Thailand restart its stalled economy.

7

NATIONS
OF
ISLANDS

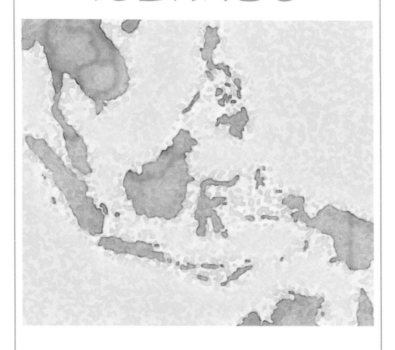

A forest of cranes stands over Jakarta, the capital of Indonesia. They are signposts of a construction boom that helped make this city one of the fastest growing in Southeast Asia—for a time. But in 1998 the cranes were motionless, marking the sites of half-built office and apartment towers where work stopped when the building bubble burst. In place of the hum of construction, the streets of Jakarta saw rioting that was sparked by a sudden plunge into economic hardship.

Indonesia, which was hard hit by the late-1990s Asian economic crisis, is one of a group of island nations that stretch from the eastern edge of the Indian Ocean to the Pacific. Singapore, Malaysia (which includes part of the Malay Peninsula), and the Philippines are among the others. They have much in common, but there are also great differences among them.

Because they lie near the equator, the island nations of Southeast Asia aren't shown accurately on many maps. The Mercator projection, for years the most common map-making method, makes countries far from the equator seem much larger than those near the line. For Americans, the map distortion has helped foster a distorted view of these countries—they're often seen as small and thus unimportant. It may help to remember that Borneo, which is governed partly by Indonesia, partly by Malaysia, and partly by the sultanate of Brunei, is the third-largest island in the world, with an area larger than Texas.

THE TINY ISLAND OF SINGAPORE, LOCATED JUST OFF THE TIP OF THE MALAY PENINSULA, IS HOME TO ONE OF THE BUSIEST HARBORS IN THE WORLD.

Size isn't everything, of course. In fact, one of the most important nations in this region, and in the entire Pacific Rim, is the smallest: tiny Singapore, less than one fourth the size of Rhode Island.

SINGAPORE

Singapore is the name of an island just 27 miles (43 kilometers) long by 14 miles (22 kilometers) wide, a nation that includes that island (along with about forty nearby islets), and a city that is the capital of that nation. What the nation lacks in size is more than made up for by two geographic blessings—an excellent natural harbor and a superb location. Singapore lies just off the tip of the Malay Peninsula, at the heart of one of the world's great shipping routes.

It was an Englishman—Thomas Stamford Raffles—who first recognized the importance of the island. At the beginning of the 1800s, a tiny fishing village was the only settlement there; but it was a natural stopping point for trading vessels passing between Europe and China. In 1819 Raffles succeeded in acquiring it from its Malay ruler for the British East India Company. Singapore grew quickly after that, and in 1867 it became a British colony. The opening of the Suez Canal in 1869 guaranteed Singapore's importance. The fastest route from Europe to the Far East was now through the canal, around the tip of India to the Bay of Bengal, and through the Strait of Malacca—to Singapore.

As a part of the British Empire, Singapore became a crossroads of international trade. Many of the people who came to live and do business in this bustling commercial center were Chinese, and people of Chinese ancestry quickly outnumbered the Malays, who were the original inhabitants. The colony's strategic location between the Indian and Pacific oceans also gave it a key role in Britain's plans for defense of its Asian territories. The British built military and naval stations on Singapore and took to calling the island the "bastion of the Empire." But the bastion's defenses were not enough to protect it in World War II. Singapore fell to the Japanese on February 15, 1942, after a six-day siege.

When the war ended and the British returned, Singapore, like other British colonies in the region, began to move toward independence. Elections for a legislature were held for the first time in 1959, and the People's Action party (PAP), a socialist group, won a clear majority. Its leader, Lee Kuan Yew, became the first prime minister. Under his leadership, in 1963, Singapore chose to merge with the newly independent federation of Malaysia. But the merger lasted less than two years. There were sharp differences between Malaysia's leaders and those of Singapore. And there were other strains—the ethnic Chinese who made up the majority of Singapore's people were viewed with suspicion by Malays elsewhere in the federation, who had long feared Chinese domination. In August 1965 Singapore left the federation and struck out on its own, as an independent state.

If Thomas Stamford Raffles was responsible for founding colonial Singapore, Lee Kuan Yew is responsible for building the modern state. In thirty years, he guided the country from relative poverty to affluence, creating something that resembles the Greek city-states of ancient times. Singapore held its position as a trade crossroads, and it became a base for financial institutions and multinational companies with Asian interests. As a result, Singapore's roughly three million people have prospered. Today about three fourths of them live in and near the capital city, where wide boulevards and gleaming office and apartment towers have replaced many of the narrow streets and crowded homes of old. Singapore is clean, efficiently run, and relatively free of crime and corruption—a great place to do business. That has helped it draw foreign investment.

But there's another side to Singapore's success story. Lee's rule is autocratic; although there are elections, and the form of government is modeled on the British parliamentary system, the PAP has never permitted opposition to take root. Critics of the government have been jailed or, often, saddled with huge libel judgments for speaking their minds. And the government's strict control extends well beyond politics. Censors check all videos that come into the country, even home videos, to make sure they contain no pornography or subversive material. Infractions like littering, taken lightly in the West, are serious in Singapore. Writing graffiti is punishable by caning— as an American teenager discovered in 1994 in a much-publicized incident. Larger crimes have devastating results. Bringing illegal drugs into the country, for example, is a capital crime.

Lee's answer to those who criticize his style of government is simple: Democracy as it is practiced in North America and Europe reflects Western values, not Asian values. The government has a duty to preserve Asian culture in the face of an onslaught of Western culture, which has made inroads in Asia in everything from clothing styles to movies and music. This argument has allowed the government to change the terms of the debate, turning the spotlight from political rights (which in the West are viewed as universal) to relative questions of culture. As one observer noted, "By misrepresenting political possibilities...as a choice between Eastern and Western cultural identities, the state can contain the threats to its power."[1]

Singaporeans have been mostly content to live with limits on their freedom as long as prosperity reigns, and Westerners have accepted the limits as the price of doing business in this thriving and efficient little country. As they feel the effects of Asia's economic downturn, however, both may chafe more at the restrictions. China has pointed to Singapore as proof that capitalism can thrive without individual rights—that discipline, not democracy, brings prosperity. It is a model the Chinese might like to adopt, in Hong Kong and elsewhere. But it's not clear that the model would work elsewhere. Singapore is so much smaller and more unified than China that comparison is impossible; and Lee has made his system function partly by avoiding the pitfalls of corruption and nepotism that plague many authoritarian governments.

MALAYSIA

A half-mile-long causeway links the island of Singapore to the Malay Peninsula and the Federation of Malaysia, across the Johor Strait. Malaysia has much in common with Singapore, including a shared history, current prosperity, and a strict government. But there are marked differences.

Malaysia is a country with thirteen states and two distinct parts. West Malaysia consists of eleven states clustered on the lower half of the Malay Peninsula, which is the heartland of the country and the site of the capital, Kuala Lumpur. East Malaysia contains two states, Sabah and Sarawak, on Borneo, several hundred miles across the South China Sea. On both the peninsula and Borneo, the land ranges from saltwater swamps along the coast to thick tropical forests and rugged mountains in the interior. Most of the people live near the coast or on rivers. West Malaysia is far more crowded than East Malaysia, much of which is wild and rugged.

In contrast to Singapore, where more than three fourths of the people are ethnic Chinese, Malaysia is an ethnic patchwork. Malays are the largest group, making up more than half the population; Bahasa Malaysia, a Malay tongue, is the country's official language. Malays are nearly all Muslims, making Islam both the official religion and an important part of daily life in the country. Ethnic Chinese make up about 30 percent of the population. Most of the Chinese live in cities, where they're often in the majority. They speak dialects of Chinese and follow Buddhism, Taoism, Christianity, and other religions. Nearly 10 percent of Malaysians are of Indian ancestry, and most of them are Hindus. Another 10 percent or so belong to native groups, such as the Dayaks, who are descended from some of the earliest inhabitants of the region. In parts of Sabah and Sarawak, these groups make up a majority.

Like Singapore, the regions that now make up Malaysia were on the path of trade routes between Europe and India and China. Islam was introduced by Arab and Indian traders, and by the thirteenth century it was firmly established as the religion of the Malays. Around 1400, Malay rulers founded the Malacca Sultanate on the western side of the peninsula. It became the most powerful of the many small Malay kingdoms and controlled the Straits of Malacca until 1511. Then the Portuguese, bent on controlling the spice trade, captured the territory. The Portuguese were in turn defeated by the Dutch, who held Malacca from the mid-1600s to 1800s and then traded it to the British. Along with Singapore and other holdings in the region, it became part of the British Straits Settlements.

The British discovered that the interior of the Malay Peninsula contained hidden riches—in the form of tin. Kuala Lumpur was founded in 1864 as a tin-mining camp. The Malay soils were mostly poor, but they turned out to be ideal for growing rubber trees, the source of natural rubber. British planters imported trees from Brazil and workers from China and India to develop huge plantations. Malaysia is still the world's largest producer of natural rubber.

Malaysia's western states were also once under British rule. In exchange for helping the sultan of Brunei put down a rebellion, the British adventurer James Brooke was made raja of Sarawak in 1841. He and his descendants ruled it for the next one hundred years. Sabah, meanwhile, came under the control of a British trading company.

All these regions fell to the Japanese in 1942. After the war, ethnic rivalries and a Communist rebellion delayed plans for independence. In 1957 the Federation of Malaya (made up of the peninsular states) finally became fully independent from Britain. Six years later, it joined with Sabah, Sarawak, and (for a time) Singapore to form the Federation of Malaysia.

From the beginning, Malaysia's biggest challenge has been balancing the interests of its various ethnic groups. There is great rivalry between the two largest groups, the Malays and ethnic Chinese. The Malays have long been fearful of Chinese domination, and they jealously guard political power. Malays hold most important government positions. Although there are more than fifteen smaller parties, the ruling United Malays National Organization has a lock on the legislature. Its leader, Datuk Seri Mahathir Mohamad, has been prime minister since 1981.

The Chinese, in turn, dominate commerce and industry. Many Malays resent this, while the Chinese resent their lack of political power. These tensions have sometimes erupted into riots. After riots killed hundreds of people in 1969, the country was placed under martial law for almost two years. Since then the government has tried to reduce tensions with a sort of affirmative action program that encourages Malays in business. It has also limited criticism of the role Malays enjoy in politics. A proponent of "Asian values," Mahathir contends that government controls must protect his country from "corrupting" Western influences. "Malaysian society still believes that freedom should not be absolute, that government has a duty to promote good values and to protect the people from the breakdown of moral and ethical standards," he explained in a 1996 speech.[2]

Exports of rubber, palm oil, and minerals—oil as well as tin—have helped Malaysia prosper. For years, the country played the role of country cousin to Singapore; but in the 1990s it began to rival Singapore as a shipping and commercial center. That, coupled with ethnic differences, has led to occasional strains between the two nations. But they remain closely linked. Singapore gets about half of its water from Malaysian sources, and Malaysian businesses and resorts draw customers from Singapore.[3]

Development is changing East Malaysia as well. Large-scale logging operations have stripped many sections of the tropical forest, and the Bakun River Dam, being built in Sarawak, will be the largest hydroelectric dam in Southeast Asia when completed. The dam project has been heavily criticized by environmental groups because it will put several thousand square miles of tropical rain forest under water, destroying wildlife habitats and displacing about ten thousand people who still follow traditional ways of life. The government has dismissed environmental criticism, however. In a situation that is not unusual in Asia's developing nations (but would clearly be a conflict of interest in the United States and most other Western nations), government officials and their relatives own shares in the company developing the dam. Sarawak's environmental minister runs a major timber operation.[4]

The dam is not the only huge construction project Malaysia has undertaken. The world's tallest building was completed in Kuala Lumpur in 1996, a monument to national pride. However, the building still had no tenants when the rising tide of Asia's economic crisis reached Malaysia in 1997. The country's currency lost 60 percent of its value on world markets, in effect destroying about $200 billion of the nation's wealth.

Prime Minister Mahathir blamed foreign speculators for the loss, although it was clear to most observers that the country faced deeper problems, including widespread corruption and banks that were overburdened with bad debts. In September 1998, with the economy in recession, Mahathir halted trading in the nation's currency and imposed rigid controls on the movement of money. Under these controls, investors were barred from pulling their money out of Malaysia for a year. In the short term, the controls stopped the continuing slide in the currency, but they did nothing for the underlying causes of the recession. In the long term, they seemed certain to scare off foreign investment.

Also in 1998 Malaysia began to deport some of the 800,000 foreign workers who had arrived when the economy was booming. Many of them were from Indonesia, where the effects of the economic slowdown were being felt even more severely.

INDONESIA

The 17,000 islands and islets that make up Indonesia stretch for 3,400 miles (5,500 kilometers), forming a long chain that links the Indian and Pacific oceans. Indonesia is the largest nation in Southeast Asia, in area and in population. In fact, with roughly 190 million people, it has the fourth-largest population in the world.

Most Indonesians are descended from Malay groups who moved into the region thousands of years ago. Chinese, Arabs, and Indians are among the minority groups.

More than two thirds of the people live on the island of Java, making that island one of the most densely populated in the world. More come from outlying islands every year, hoping to find jobs in Jakarta and other cities. The government offers jobs and other incentives to get people to move from Java to outlying islands, but it hasn't been able to reverse the trend. In remote provinces like Irian Jaya (on New Guinea) and Kalimantan (on Borneo) there's plenty of room, but life is much harder.

More than 85 percent of Indonesians are Muslims, making this one of the world's most important Muslim countries. Minority religions include Hinduism, which survives mainly on the island of Bali; and Christianity and Buddhism, both followed by many ethnic Chinese. Hindu stories play a role in traditional arts that are enjoyed by Indonesians of all faiths—Javanese puppet plays, various dances, and Balinese folk operas.

Trade shaped Indonesia's unique cultural mix. The islands lie on the path between China and India, and in early times they were the source of sought-after spices. (The Moluccas, the fabled Spice Islands, are part of the Indonesian group.) Small Hindu and Buddhist kingdoms flourished on Java and Sumatra as early as the second century. In the 1300s much of what is today Indonesia came under Javanese rule. Later, Java became a center for Islam, which arrived with Arab traders and spread throughout the islands. Europeans also called at Indonesian ports, drawn by the lucrative spice trade. The Portuguese built several trading posts in the islands, but they were eventually driven out everywhere except the eastern part of the island of Timor.

It was the Dutch who came to dominate Indonesia, first through the commercial empire of the Dutch East India Company and, after 1798, colonial rule. Governing the scattered islands was a challenge, and the Dutch never really controlled all of them. They focused on Java and other key locations, and they put down repeated rebellions. But the restrictions imposed by the Dutch eventually backfired, promoting a growing sense of nationalism in Indonesia. By the 1920s there was a real nationalist movement, led by such groups as the Islamic Union, the Indonesian Communist party (PKI), and the Indonesian Nationalist party (PNI). Indonesians resented Dutch control so much that many actually welcomed the Japanese forces that overran the islands in World War II. After the war, when the Dutch tried to reestablish control, they faced a full-scale revolution. In 1949 they were forced to recognize Indonesia's independence.

Two leaders have had profound influences on Indonesia since then. Sukarno, president from 1949 to 1967, was a leader in the independence movement. (Like many Indonesians, Sukarno went by a single name.) In 1960 he dissolved the legislature and instituted a policy called "guided democracy," which regulated political parties. Sukarno became increasingly anti-Western in outlook, aligning himself with the PKI and developing ties with the Soviet Union and China. He vehemently opposed the formation of Malaysia, and in 1965 he withdrew Indonesia from the United Nations. The country seemed likely to join the Communist bloc—until the Indonesian Communists tried to speed things up by seizing power. The attempt failed and prompted a reaction in which army-backed vigilantes killed several hundred thousand suspected Communist sympathizers.

In the turmoil that followed, Sukarno was stripped of power, and a new government, led by General Suharto, was formed. Suharto reversed many of Sukarno's policies, taking the country back into the United Nations and renewing ties with the West. Hoping to position Indonesia as a diplomatic and commercial leader in the region, he played a key role in founding ASEAN, the economic and trade association that initially included

Malaysia, Singapore, the Philippines, Thailand, and Brunei and later grew to include other nations. ASEAN has helped the small nations of Southeast Asia stand up to economic giants like China and Japan, and it has fueled the region's remarkable economic growth.

Oil and gas reserves helped Indonesia's economy grow, and the standard of living rose for many people. But the country faced many problems, including sporadic rebellions on outlying islands. Perhaps the most troubling situation developed after Indonesia took over the former Portuguese colony of East Timor 1975. East Timorese resistance has never stopped, and Indonesia has been accused of widespread violations of human rights on the island. In 1996 two outspoken critics of the takeover, Bishop Carlos Filipe Ximenes Belo and José Ramos-Horta, won the Nobel Peace Prize.

Ethnic violence is another persistent problem in Indonesia. As in Malaysia, many ethnic Chinese have been successful in business, and this provokes resentment. Sometimes the resentment boils over into anti-Chinese riots. Early in 1997, for example, a series of riots destroyed Chinese shops, homes, temples, and churches in several Javanese towns. In many cases the trigger for rioting was nothing more than gossip or an imagined insult.

Riots also preceded national elections in 1997, in which Suharto's party, Golkar, won 74 percent of the vote. The results surprised no one, since opposition rallies had been blocked and millions of civil servants and people in the military were required to vote for Golkar. But many observers noted that discontent was growing, due in large part to a widening gap between rich and poor and to limits on political freedom. Many of the rioters who hurled rocks in the weeks before the vote were young people from the poorest levels of society. An Indonesian psychologist noted: "Many of them are jobless, or work as servants, coolies, or thugs. They don't have any idea of what politics is."[5]

Corruption and nepotism were another source of dissatisfaction. In the thirty-plus years of Suharto's rule, the president's children and close supporters had built up huge business empires, based on concessions doled out by the government. They acquired stakes in mining, manufacturing, banking, and just about every other aspect of business. In all, the holdings were worth anywhere from $5 to $15 billion.

This "crony capitalism" was one of the factors that made Indonesia a flash point of the 1997–1998 Asian economic crisis. Indonesian banks and businesses had borrowed heavily abroad, and much of the money wasn't well managed. When Thailand's economy collapsed in mid-1997, investors took another look at Indonesia and decided that the risks there were too high. They began to pull their money out, and as a result the value of the country's currency plunged 70 percent—and the loans could not be repaid. Indonesia turned to the International Monetary Fund, which put together a $43 billion aid package. But to get it, Indonesia was required to reform its economy—to regulate its banks, end subsidies for fuel and food, break up some of the family business empires, and make other changes. Suharto balked, and many Indonesians supported him because the IMF requirements smacked of colonial rule. In the end, both sides compromised, with the IMF doling out aid slowly in exchange for piecemeal reforms.

But the IMF aid—and even an additional $1 billion pledged by the United States—would not be enough to solve Indonesia's problems. The downturn meant that more Indonesians were out of work, increasing the chances of unrest. In May 1998, as prices for fuel and food began to rise, students and others once again took to the streets. Rioting spread from outlying towns to the capital. When soldiers fired on a crowd of protesters, killing several young people, Indonesians were outraged. More people joined the demonstrations. The shops and businesses of ethnic Chinese were burned and looted, and businesses owned by Suharto's children and friends were also targeted. At least five hundred people were killed.

Suharto, now in his seventies, clearly seemed to have lost control of the country. On May 21 he resigned. Bacharuddin Jusef Habibie, his vice president and long-time protégé, was sworn in to replace him. To quell the unrest, Habibie promised to hold elections and to weed out the corruption and favoritism that had plagued the Suharto years. Indonesians seemed willing to give him the chance to make good on his word. But the country's future was uncertain. The economy was still in tatters, and some observers wondered whether growing ethnic and religious tensions would tear Indonesia apart.

THE PHILIPPINES

Northeast of Indonesia and Malaysia lies another group of islands—the Philippines—with a history and traditions that are markedly different from those of its neighbors. Yet the people of the Philippines have faced many of the same problems, and their success is a promising sign for the region.

The seven thousand islands of the Philippines are mostly small and uninhabited; a handful of large islands are home to most of the people. The largest and most important is Luzon, site of Manila, the capital. The islands were settled by waves of immigrants who arrived over centuries, mainly from the Malay and Indonesian islands but also from China and other regions. As in Indonesia and Malaysia, a variety of ethnic groups live in the Philippines today. There are ten major languages, although Filipino (the official national language) and English are spoken widely. More than 90 percent of Filipinos are Christians, chiefly Roman Catholics; Muslims and Buddhists are minorities.

The influence of the West has been far stronger in the Philippines than elsewhere in Southeast Asia. The islands were a colony of Spain for more than three hundred years, from the mid-1500s to the late 1800s. Spanish rule brought the Roman Catholic religion, the European calendar and alphabet, and a Western way of life. The benefits were mainly enjoyed by a handful of wealthy families, however. Average Filipinos worked hard for their colonial rulers, with little compensation and no political freedom. As a result, the Philippines became the site of the first nationalist movement in Southeast Asia. After José Rizal, a leader of the movement, was executed in 1896, rebellion broke out.

The Spanish were struggling to put down the revolt and hang on to the islands when the Spanish-American War began in 1898. Although the war's prime causes (and most of the fighting) were halfway around the world in Cuba, the Philippines was involved. A United States fleet under Commodore George Dewey defeated the Spanish fleet in Manila Bay on May 1. Filipino partisans then worked with the U.S. forces to take control of the islands. The Filipino leader Emilio Aguinaldo declared the Philippines independent, but the treaty that ended the Spanish-American War ceded the islands to the United States. Aguinaldo's forces fought the Americans for several years, but eventually he was captured.

Saying that it would rule the islands only until they were ready for independence, the United States set up a system of public schools and oversaw the development of a democratic constitution. In 1935 the self-governing Philippine Commonwealth was formed. But the Philippines were one of the first targets for Japanese attack in

World War II, and the islands fell in May 1942. After the war, the Philippines regained freedom and reorganized as a republic. The United States maintained several large military bases on the islands, so U.S. influence remained strong.

After a series of separatist rebellions in the 1960s, Philippine president Ferdinand Marcos placed the country under martial law. During his twenty years in power, Marcos, his family, and his supporters developed their own brand of corrupt crony capitalism, fleecing the country and stashing billions of dollars in foreign bank accounts. As a result, the Philippines largely missed out on Asia's economic boom.

When Marcos was finally overthrown in 1986, strikes and unrest continued to scare off foreign investors. But by the early 1990s, things had begun to change. The government addressed some of the worst problems hindering growth—such as inadequate power supplies that made brownouts and blackouts common. Under an IMF-supervised program, it ended monopolies in the airline, banking, and other industries. The economy began to grow slowly but steadily. As a result, when economic crises hit other Asian countries, the Philippines was in a strong position. Stocks and currency lost value, but banks stayed profitable because they weren't saddled with bad loans. Construction, which ground to a halt in Thailand and Indonesia, continued because builders hadn't over-built—there were no empty office towers in Manila.

The Philippines still faces many problems, including severe poverty in the bottom rungs of society. But for a country that once seemed to have been left in the dust by the rapid development of its neighbors, a conservative and cautious approach to growth seems to be working. As one Filipino businessman remarked, "There's a bit of truth to the case of the turtle and the hare."[6]

8
EAST ASIA AND THE PACIFIC

A NEW VIEW

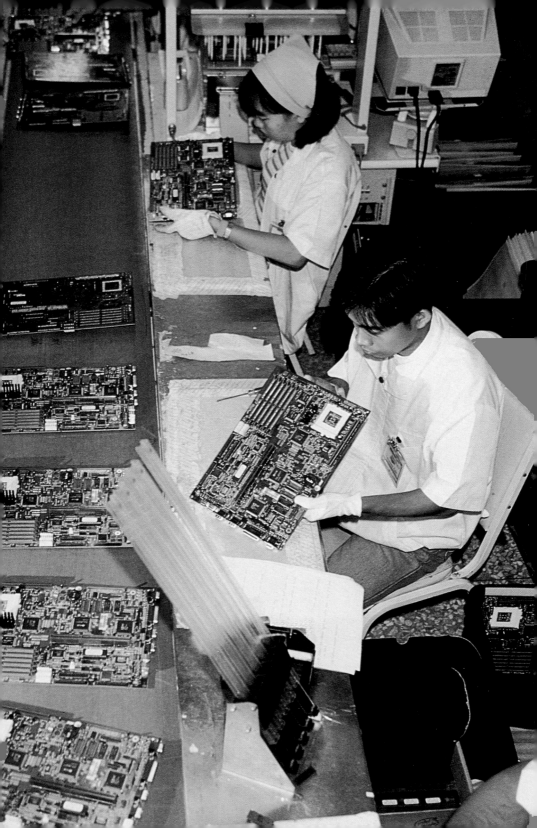

Before economic troubles reined in East Asian growth, the region was one of the most exciting and important places to do business in the world, especially for American companies. In the mid-1990s, East Asian and Pacific nations together accounted for more than $424 billion in trade with the United States—70 percent more than U.S. trade with European nations. Moreover, Americans had invested more than $108 billion in the region.[1] That was before Asian currencies and stock markets plunged in 1997. Still, most people expected the region to rebound.

Because East Asia had become so important, the United States and other Western countries backed record amounts of aid from the IMF to the most severely hit countries to keep them from defaulting on their debts. The aid came with conditions: In exchange for billions of dollars in loans and guarantees, the IMF asked Thailand, South Korea, and Indonesia to cut public spending, limit credit, lower barriers to foreign trade and investment, end subsidies for inefficient industries, break up monopolies, and take action against corruption.

By ending some of the practices that led to the economic problems, these and similar steps were meant to

EAST ASIA IS A SOURCE OF INEXPENSIVE LABOR, AND U.S. COMPANIES HAVE INVESTED HEAVILY IN INDUSTRY THERE. THE AREA IS ALSO A MAJOR TRADING PARTNER FOR THE UNITED STATES. EAST ASIAN POLITICAL AND FINANCIAL UNREST CAN BE A CAUSE OF CONCERN THROUGHOUT MUCH OF THE WESTERN WORLD.

restore confidence in the financial institutions and governments of these countries, and to put their economies on firmer footing. Initially, however, many Asians thought the conditions would only make life harder by increasing business bankruptcies and unemployment. Many saw the requirements as a new sort of Western colonialism or a guise through which the United States would get the open markets it had been demanding. The outcry was so great in Indonesia that the agency was forced to ease its requirements. But in Thailand and South Korea, currency and stock markets stopped their dramatic fall once the IMF program was accepted.

Many analysts expected the worst of the economic "Asian flu" to be quickly over. By mid-1998, they had to revise their estimates. Indonesia, Malaysia, South Korea, and Thailand were still suffering, and they had been joined by Japan. Hong Kong was in a slump. Even countries where the economy had managed to keep growing—China, the Philippines, Singapore, and Taiwan—were feeling the effects of the flu. A regional recession was in full swing, and its effects were felt worldwide as companies that did business in Asia saw their profits evaporating.

Recovery may take time, but it should come, most analysts agree. Even though the late-1990s troubles put a chill on investment and trade, the fundamentals that contributed to the East Asian success story haven't changed. Even the drop in value of Asian currencies may have a silver lining for these countries: Their products have become cheaper on world markets, so their exports are likely to increase. That should lead to more employment. And these nations still have the basic advantages that fueled their boom of the 1980s, including well-educated and highly motivated workers.

Not all the questions confronting East Asia and the Pacific are economic, however. Many of these nations are faced with issues of political freedom within their borders, and regional issues involving security and international relations. All these issues are intertwined with the region's economic outlook. The healthier the economy of the region, the easier they will be to solve. And the sooner they are solved, the healthier the economy will be.

POLITICAL FREEDOM

So-called "Asian values" have been cast in a new light by the economic crisis. In flush times, authoritarian governments like those in Indonesia and Singapore were tolerated in the West. In the face of the overwhelming economic success of the region, it was hard to argue with their rulers' assertions that democracy and human rights were alien "Western" concepts that would be unnecessary and even harmful to Asian nations. Some Western business leaders even praised these autocratic governments, which seemed so much more efficient than democracies. Human-rights abuses drew protests from Western governments—but the protests were often muted, in the interest of maintaining good trade relations, and just as often brushed aside.

After 1997, however, it was clear to many observers that lack of democracy was partly responsible for the economic misery in countries such as Indonesia and Thailand. Martin Lee, leader of the Hong Kong Democratic party and a prominent advocate for democracy in the region, wrote: "It is no accident that Indonesia is now suffering the most from the Asian financial flu. Its causes? A despotic ruler who learned to cash in on his absolute political control, investors who relied on cronyism instead of market forces, and a lack of accountability and common-sense financial controls." In contrast, the countries that weathered the storm best—Taiwan, the Philippines, and Japan—were the most democratic. Lee was among those who urged Western nations to attach conditions for political reform, as well as economic reform, to Asian aid and loans. "A government that is not answerable to its people will not be likely to have open markets or the institutions required to impose discipline to overcome a financial crisis," he said.[2]

As we've seen in earlier chapters, pressure for political reform came from within East Asian nations, as well as from the West, in the wake of the economic crisis. In South Korea and Thailand, corrupt regimes were voted out. In Indonesia, riots and protests drove Suharto from office.

Greater democracy and political freedom may turn out to be another silver lining to the economic crisis. Even China—the region's most repressive nation and the one least influenced by Western opinion—may feel the indirect effects of reform. At the least, Chinese leaders can no longer point to neighboring countries as proof of the claim that discipline, not democracy, is the formula for success.

SECURITY

Unlike the nations of Europe, which banded together with the United States to form the North Atlantic Treaty Organization after World War II, East Asian nations didn't develop a strong regional military alliance during the Cold War years. The South East Asia Treaty Organization (SEATO), meant to be a counterpart to NATO, was only a shadow of the European organization. But the United States has maintained a continuous military presence in the Pacific from the end of World War II to the present. During the Cold War, the Pacific forces were part of a global strategy focused on preventing the spread of communism. In the 1990s, after the breakup of the Soviet Union, U.S. forces stayed to help ensure stability in the region and to reassure close allies, particularly Japan and South Korea, of continued U.S. support.

The United States remains the region's strongest shield against its two greatest security threats. China is a nuclear power with tremendous military potential, and it has shown in its actions toward Taiwan how willing it is to throw its armed weight around. North Korea, which badly wants to be a nuclear power, continues to threaten South Korea. Moreover, China, Korea, Japan, and several Southeast Asian nations are involved in long-running territorial disputes and competition for undersea mineral resources. Any one of these potential conflicts could erupt at any time. The U.S. military presence is a deterrent to conflict, as well as a counterweight to Chinese power.

Today, however, the U.S. military presence is a subject of debate on both sides of the Pacific. No one is suggesting that the United States should withdraw its forces completely from the East Asia. Without strong armies of their own, Japan and other U.S. allies in the region need the American military. But American troops and bases in Asia have been the targets of resentment and protests. Local resentment was a factor in the closing of two U.S. bases in the Philippines—Subic Bay Naval Base and Clark Air Force Base—in 1992. Three years later a serious situation developed in Japan, after U.S. servicemen stationed on the island of Okinawa raped a twelve-year-old girl. Japanese protesters demanded that U.S. troops be withdrawn. That didn't happen, although one base on Okinawa was closed.

The U.S. government has also faced domestic pressure to reduce its Pacific forces. The umbrella of security provided by the United States was one of many factors that helped Japan (which under its postwar constitution was prevented from developing strong military forces) and other East Asian nations to flourish. In the 1980s, at the height of Japan's phenomenal economic growth, some Americans resented the fact that Japan spent little on its own defense while the United States had a huge military budget. "The Cold War is over, and Japan won," was a widely quoted quip.[3] Since then the U.S. government has encouraged Japan and other nations to take on a larger share of their own defense obligations and to work together to solve regional disputes.

EAST AND WEST

In 1989 a member of the Japanese parliament asserted that there was "no hope" for the United States. Western civilization was nearing its end, he confidently stated, and the future belonged to Asia.[4] It was a view that was widely shared, although seldom expressed so bluntly. American business experts in the 1980s rushed to study the Japanese system, to discover the secrets of its success.

Ten years later, the balance had shifted. As East Asian countries struggled with their economic problems, the United States was enjoying good times, with low unemployment and soaring stock prices. Americans were inclined to pat themselves on the back—just as some Japanese had congratulated themselves a few years earlier. But with trade and security links reaching across the Pacific, it was clear that the United States and other Pacific Rim nations would feel the effects of East Asia's troubles.

The U.S. balance of trade was affected directly. Trade deficits have been a major irritant in relations between the United States and Asian nations, especially Japan. The United States is the single largest market for exports from these countries, annually importing goods worth far more than those it exports to them. By spending more on imports than they earn on exports, Americans have built up huge trade deficits. In 1994, for example, the U.S. trade deficit with Japan was more than $65 billion; with China, nearly $30 billion.[5] United States officials have long complained that Japan, South Korea, Taiwan, and other big exporters used trade barriers—taxes, quotas, and other devices—to keep foreign goods out.

In the mid-1990s, American negotiators won agreements from several of these nations to lower trade barriers. At the same time, the value of these nations' currencies was rising on world markets. That had the effect of making their products more expensive—and thus less attractive—in America. The U.S. annual trade deficits began to shrink. But when Asian currencies tumbled in value in 1997, the trend reversed. From cars and clothing to television sets, Asian imports dropped in price, so more Americans could afford them. At the same time, hard-pressed consumers in Asian countries could no longer buy American goods.

The first result of the shift was that the U.S. trade deficit rose again. Analysts expected more repercussions down the road. With stiffer competition from Asian goods at home, and a shrinking market for U.S. goods abroad, profits at American companies seemed likely to slip. If U.S. firms began to lay off workers, unemployment would rise, and the U.S. economy would slow down. The hope of warding off this threat was a major reason why many American business leaders urged the U.S. Congress to increase funding for the IMF in 1998. Nevertheless, worry that the Asian recession might spread helped send the U.S. stock markets down sharply in the summer of 1998.

American businesses also went looking for other markets. The countries of Latin America were high on the list, and stronger trade links with that region were another possible outcome of East Asia's downturn. But ties across the Pacific remain strong all the same. Whatever changes in fortune may come, the futures of the Pacific nations are linked by common interests. Open markets, political freedom, and peace and stability will benefit them all.

SOURCE NOTES

CHAPTER I

1. Robert H. Burgess, ed., *The Sea Serpent Journal: Hugh McCulloch Gregory's Voyage Around the World by Clipper Ship, 1854–55* (Charlottesville: University Press of Virginia, 1975), p. 85.
2. James C. Thomson, Jr., Peter W. Stanley, and John Curtis Perry, *Sentimental Imperialists: The American Experience in East Asia* (New York: Harper & Row, 1981), p. 47.

CHAPTER 2

1. Arnold Brackman, *The Other Nuremberg: The Untold Story of the Tokyo War Crimes Trials* (New York: William Morrow, 1987), p. 78.
2. For an in-depth look at contemporary Japanese business, see Nobura Yoshimura and Philip Anderson, *Inside the Kaisha: Demystifying Japanese Business Behavior* (Boston: Harvard Business School Press, 1997).
3. Nicholas D. Kristof, "Where Children Rule," *The New York Times Magazine*, August 17, 1997, p. 40.
4. Okano Yutaka, "Twenty Years of Frustration," Japan File (www.kto.co.jp).
5. Kristof, "Stateside Lingo Gives Japan Its Own Valley Girls," *The New York Times*, October 19, 1997.

6. Sheryl WuDunn, "In Japan, Old Problem Undermines New Leaders," *The New York Times*, November 23, 1996.
7. Charles Lane, "Re-orient," *The New Republic*, May 20, 1996, p. 6.
8. Sebastian Mallaby, "Uneasy Partners," *The New York Times Book Review*, September 21, 1997, p. 34.

CHAPTER 3

1. Erik Eckholm, "Delectable Materialism Catching On in China," *The New York Times*, January 10, 1998.
2. Eckholm, "Joblessness: A Perilous Curve on China's Capitalist Road," *The New York Times*, January 20, 1998.
3. Eckholm, "New China Leader Promises Reforms for Every Sector," *The New York Times*, March 20, 1998.
4. John Greenwald, "Get Asia Now, Pay Later," *Time*, October 10, 1994, p. 61.
5. Patrick E. Tyler, "A Democrat in China: Like an Egg Against a Rock," *The New York Times*, February 6, 1997.
6. Eckholm, "New China Leader."

CHAPTER 4

1. Edward A. Gargan, "Bowed, Not Battered," *The New York Times*, February 24, 1998.
2. Patrick E. Tyler, "The China-and-Taiwan Problem," *The New York Times*, February 11, 1996.

CHAPTER 5

1. Ron Gluckman, "Life in Paradise," *Asiaweek*, September 1991.
2. Excerpts from a speech given by Kim Jong Il on May 5, 1991, quoted in *A Handbook on North Korea*, (*Korea Herald*, 1996).
3. Gluckman, "Life in Paradise."

CHAPTER 6

1. Seth Mydans, "Signs of Recovery, but the Hard-Hit Brace for an 'Ugly' Year, *The New York Times*, January 5, 1998.
2. Frank Gibney, "Back in Business," *Time*, April 24, 1995.
3. Seth Mydans, "Thailand Economic Crash Crushes Working Poor," *The New York Times*, December 15, 1997.

CHAPTER 7

1. Janandas Devan, "The Singapore Way," *The New York Review of Books*, June 6, 1996.
2. Seth Mydans, "Hard Times Weaken a Malaysian Powerbroker," *The New York Times*, October 21, 1997.
3. S. Jayasankaran and Murray Hiebert, "Snipe, Snipe," *Far Eastern Economic Review*, June 5, 1997.
4. Dennis Schulz, "An Unholy Alliance in East Malaysia," *World Press Review*, August 1997 (reprinted from *The Australian*, May 10–11, 1997).
5. Margot Cohen, "Blowing the Lid," *Far Eastern Economic Review*, May 29, 1997.
6. Edward A. Gargan, "Last Laugh for the Philippines," *The New York Times*, December 11, 1997.

CHAPTER 8

1. US Department of State Fact Sheet, "U.S. Economic Relations with East Asia and the Pacific," *US Department of State Dispatch*, vol. 6, November 20, 1985, p. 855.
2. Martin Lee, "Testing Asian Values," *The New York Times*, January 18, 1998.
3. Nicholas D. Kristoff, "Hubris and Humility as U.S. Waxes and Asia Wanes," *The New York Times*, March 22, 1998.
4. *Ibid.*
5. US Department of State Fact Sheet.

FURTHER READING

Brackman, Arnold. *The Other Nuremberg: The Untold Story of the Tokyo War Crimes Trials*. New York: William Morrow, 1984.

Carter, Alden R. *China Past—China Future*. New York: Franklin Watts, 1994.

Detzer, David. *An Asian Tragedy: America and Vietnam*. Brookfield, CT: Millbrook Press, 1992.

Downer, Lesley. *Japan*. Chatham, NJ: Steck-Vaughn, 1995.

Garten, Jeffrey. *The Big Ten: The Big Emerging Markets and How They Will Change Our Lives*. New York: Basic Books, 1997.

Gibney, Frank. *The Pacific Century: America and Asia in a Changing World*. New York: Charles Scribner's Sons, 1992.

Gyatso, Palden. *The Autobiography of a Tibetan Monk*. New York: Grove Press, 1997.

Kort, Michael. *China Under Communism*. Brookfield, CT: Millbrook Press, 1995.

Meyer, Carolyn. *A Voice From Japan: An Outsider Looks In.* San Diego: Harcourt Brace, 1992.

Naisbitt, John. *Megatrends Asia: Eight Asian Megatrends That Are Reshaping Our World.* New York: Simon & Schuster, 1996.

Thompson, James C., Jr., and Peter W. Stanley and John Curtis Perry. *Sentimental Imperialists: The American Experience in East Asia.* New York: Harper & Row, 1981.

Wu, Harry, with George Vecsey. *Troublemaker: One Man's Crusade Against China's Cruelty.* New York: Times Books/ Random House, 1997.

INDEX

Page numbers in *italics* refer to illustrations.

agriculture
  China, *42*, 44–45
  Japan, 26
Aguinaldo, Emilio, 109

Boxer Rebellion, 20
Brooke, James, 101

Cambodia, 85, 87–89
Chiang Ching-kuo, 65
Chiang Kai-shek, 49, *60*, 61, 62, 65
China, 7, 41–57
  agriculture, *42*, 44–45
  Boxer Rebellion, 20
  culture, 14–15, 46
  democracy and human rights, 53–55
  economy and trade, 13–15, 43–44, 50–53, 114
  education, 49, 50
  ethnic groups, 46–47
  family and community, 47–48
  missionaries, 16–17
  People's Republic of, 49–55, 61–63
  population, 44
  rivers, 45–46

China *(continued)*
  spheres of interest, 19
  Taiwan and, 61–63, 66–68, 117
Chinese immigrants, 17–18
Chuan Leekpai, 91
Chun Doo Hwan, 74
Clinton, Bill, 56, 67
communism, 21, 37
  in Cambodia, 88
  in China, 49–55
  in Indonesia, 105
  in North Korea, 76
  in Vietnam, 85–86
Confucius, 47

Dalai Lama, 47
democracy, 53–56, 74–75, 91, 92, 98, 99, 115
Deng Xiaoping, 50, 51
Dewey, George, 109

economy and trade
  China, 13–15, 43–44, 50–53, 114
  Indonesia, 8, 95, 104–107, 115, 116
  Japan, 7, 14, 25, 27, 30–31, 34–35, 38–39, 116, 118, 119
  Koreas, 8, 71, 73, 75, 77–78, 114, 119